Costume Reference 8

1918-1939

MARION SICHEL

B.T. Batsford London

First published 1978

ISBN 0 7134 1136 8

Typeset by Tek-Art Ltd
Printed in Great Britain by
The Anchor Press Ltd, Tiptree, Essex
for the publishers B.T. Batsford Ltd,
4 Fitzhardinge Street, London W1H 0AH

Contents

5 Introduction

7 Men
24 Women
63 Children

65 Glossary
69 Select Bibliography
71 Index

On the left the dinner dress is with a yoked waist and gathered bodice. The sleeves are gathered at the top to give a square look. The central figure is of a man in the uniform of the Royal Air Force. The lady on the right is wearing a casual suit, its square look and the padded shoulders on the jacket giving a masculine appearance. The wide slacks have turn-ups, c. 1939

Introduction

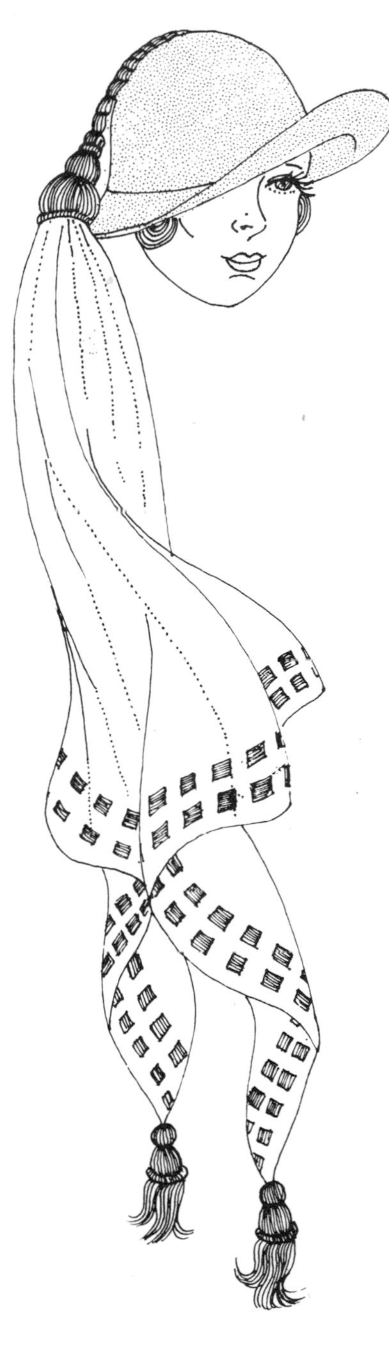

The period between the two World Wars, 1918-1939, saw great fluctuations in the world of fashion. Both men's and women's fashions reflected, perhaps to a greater extent than ever before, the great changes taking place in society and in the outlook of the time: the levelling of classes, the decrease in formality and, for women, the move towards emancipation.

For men, frock coats and morning coats moved into the field of purely formal wear and lounge suits became more usual – perhaps in a dark material with striped trousers for business. Casual clothes came to the fore generally; plus fours, Fair Isle sweaters instead of waistcoats, loose flannel trousers, fringed brogued shoes, and soft Trilby or snap brim hats rather than the top hat. The casual look was exemplified in one of the most extreme modes of this period – the Oxford bags, baggy flared trousers whose turn-ups in 1925 reached 60 cm in width!

Women's fashions reflected the new freedom enjoyed by women after the First World War. Skirts became straighter and then shorter, revealing the knees by 1925-27, this being the shortest style so far in the history of fashion. The waistline disappeared and the bustline was abolished. A shorter, straighter silhouette was the thing. Hairstyles followed this masculine trend with bobs, shingles and Eton crops. Then the tide turned and in the 1930s women's clothes became softer and longer again, with skirts often gored or cut on the cross. Hair was grown longer and hats became bigger and more romantic. Certain 'masculine' touches did however remain to influence clothes such as the popular swagger and trench coats and the square-shouldered tailor-mades. Women's fashions had come a long way from the restrictive styles, such as the barrel-shaped skirts, of the beginning of our period.

The faster and more frequent changes in fashion between the wars were both caused and made possible by the great increase in the ready-to-wear trade, in machine-made goods in particular. This meant that it was not only the upper classes who could keep up with fashion, so as a result fashion leaders demanded ever-new styles to stay ahead.

Our period also displayed a greater variety in types of clothes worn and in the materials used in their manufacture. Knitted goods came in for the first time – jumpers, twin sets, berets, even the new two-piece bathing costumes. Pyjamas, in artificial silk, became acceptable for cocktail wear and shorts on the beach or for tennis. Headwear multiplied – snoods, turbans and pillboxes were all popular – and, still in the field of accessories, platform-soled and wedge-heeled shoes were crazes, and wrist rather than pocket watches became established. Suede was used for shoes and crêpe and rubber for their soles, string and leather for gloves, rubberised cotton for raincoats, zips instead of straps and buckles for trousers.

The mood of excitement and movement was brought to an end by the Second World War and the consequent clampdown on fashion with the diversion of resources into war production and the restrictions of clothes rationing. Looking back, however, over our period, it is interesting to see just how much fashion had altered, in the way it was viewed as much as in individual styles and waves of popularity. Fashion was for everybody – not solely for an élite – and it was to stay that way.

Men

Oxford bags, although grossly exaggerated, set the fashion for wider trousers of the future, c. 1925

About 1924-25 trousers became extremely wide. Oxford undergraduates set the fashion by wearing trousers so widely cut that only the tips of their shoes were visible. This mode did not last long in its most extreme form and by the end of the decade Oxford bags, as they were known, had settled down to having just fairly wide bottoms. These were worn until the end of the 1930s.

Meanwhile *knickerbockers* enjoyed a renewed spell in fashion, being popularised by the baggy breeches of the First World War Guards officers. The new knickerbockers were cut even more amply and were known as plus fours – they hung over the top of the puttees to four inches below the knee. Plus fours became very popular for golf and country pursuits, leaving the old knickerbocker costume to be worn by old-fashioned intellectuals.

The Prince of Wales, later King Edward VIII, led the fashion in men's wear. He popularised Oxford bags and plus fours, as well as Prince of Wales checks and tweeds. He also introduced and made popular 'Fair Isle' sweaters, which began to replace waistcoats, although white waistcoats were still worn with dinner jackets.

As the fashion for waistcoats declined, so double-breasted coats became more usual. Single-breasted coats were still worn, however, and by the late 1920s double-breasted waistcoats had come into fashion again.

For ordinary town wear *lounge suits* were worn, but from about 1922 the jackets became shorter and the slit at the back was omitted. Jacket lapels became wider and as the width of a tie blade always corresponded with the width of the lapel, so ties became wider also.

After the end of the First World War *frock coats* ceased to be fashionable, whilst morning coats remained in vogue for funerals and weddings.

FROCK COATS

Frock coats were worn on formal occasions, and by the late 1920s were also worn at funerals instead of morning coats, although George V wore them frequently. Frock coats were generally double breasted with two to three buttons either side and an extra buttonhole on each lapel. Button stands were sewn to the front edges. The rolled lapels usually reached the buttons and were faced with silk. The coats had a centre back vent with pleats either side which would contain pockets. The top of the back vent had two buttons at the head. Sometimes a ticket pocket was inserted at the waist seam and a breast pocket could be on the inside or the outside. The straight sleeves might be cuffed and edged with a flat braid to match the coat fronts and lapel edges. If the cuffs were of the slit variety they also had buttons. The frock coats were slightly longer waisted than they had been in the late 1890s, and were usually worn open.

Waistcoats worn with frock coats were more often double breasted with lapels and occasionally also a collar. They were sometimes of the same colour as, or slightly lighter than, the coats with which they were worn.

Trousers were made to match the outfit or were made of a striped material.

MORNING COATS

Morning coats were invariably single breasted with three to four buttons or just one link button. The front skirts were cut away more than those of the previous period so that the tails at the back appeared narrower. Step collars made at right-angles and broad lapels were fashionable, but braid decoration was little used. By about 1923 the tails also became a little shorter. Outside flap pockets gradually began to make their appearance. These coats were mainly worn for formal occasions such as weddings.

Morning coats in the 1920s were lined with a black silk and cotton mixture, whilst the sleeves were lined in a different material, usually a checked shiny cotton. Below and around the armholes the linings were often quilted. If the sleeves were cuffed, they were of the slit variety with three buttons. The back of the coat had a central vent with a

Spring fashion coat and top hat, c. 1920

pleat either side which had a button sewn at the top. There were generally pockets in the pleats as well as inside the front of the coat. One outside pocket was generally on the left breast to hold a handkerchief. Collars were usually of the step variety with long lapels reaching the buttons. In the left side lapel there was generally a buttonhole to hold a flower.

From the mid-1920s morning coats had notched lapels which could either be fairly wide or pointed. The most popular fashion of fastening became the one link button at the waist. The fronts of the coat sloped back quite sharply to narrower tails than previously, and the edges were sometimes braided.

Morning coats worn with grey waistcoats, striped trousers and silk top hats, mainly for ceremonial occasions and weddings, were very often hired.

Waistcoats worn with morning coats were single breasted, although very rarely double-breasted styles were worn. They were usually without collars and made in the same material as the coat. The backs were tightened with a strap and buckle. The backs of waistcoats were made in a cheaper material, usually a cotton and silk mixture or satin, whilst the fronts were lined in a shiny cotton, often of a checked pattern.

Trousers were of a striped grey or black and white cashmere material, but if the outfit was worn as a morning suit, trousers, waistcoat and coat were all made to match. Tweeds and checks were popular, mainly in grey or dark materials. The trousers were so made that they were held up with braces, the back being higher to accommodate the brace buttons and also a strap and buckle to adjust the waist measurement. Pockets were often inserted in the side seams of trousers. The fronts of the trousers were closed with buttons and buttonholes covered by a fly. A metal hook and bar would fasten them at the waist.

Silk hats were the usual headwear, although Homburgs and bowlers could also be worn.

Lounge suit and Homburg hat, c. 1924

LOUNGE SUITS

Lounge jackets were shorter than before the First World War. Very often there were buttonholes on each lapel, the left one used to hold a flower. Lounge coats were usually single breasted with two to four buttons. A back vent could be present but was not essential. The coats were made to fit the shape of the body by darting the side fronts to the top of the side pockets. Double-breasted lounge jackets, when the back was cut without a centre seam, merged in style with reefer coats, although they were less popular than the single-breasted styles.

Reefer jackets, usually double breasted, had up to eight buttons, whilst the single-breasted types had only four. They always had square cut fronts and no back seam, and were worn closed. The Reefer style soon merged with the lounge jacket.

About 1923 when double-breasted lounge jackets were worn they had about six buttons, rolled lapels and two waist and one breast pockets. The sleeve cuffs had two buttons and the jackets had a central back vent. White waistcoats and checked trousers were usual with this style.

The single-breasted jackets, until about 1925, had one to three buttons. The lapels varied in shape and angle and there were usually three outside pockets, the hip pocket generally being flapped and perhaps with piping along the open edges.

After about 1925 lounge suits became the most popular men's wear. They were worn on all kinds of occasions, even when in the past formal attire had been essential. They consisted of jacket, waistcoat and trousers, but by about 1937 waistcoats were generally no longer worn for informal and weekend wear. The trousers could then be of a different shade to the jacket.

With the declining popularity of frock and morning coats for general wear, lounge suit jackets and waistcoats tended to be made in black or dark grey materials and worn with striped trousers. These suits were worn by both professional and business men.

About 1926 lounge jackets acquired a definite waistline and three outside pockets. The sleeve cuffs usually had three buttons. If jackets were single breasted, the revers were of the roll variety and were not pressed down. Although three buttons were present down the front only the middle one was done up. The fronts of the jacket were usually rounded at the hem, but by about 1928 they were often straight and square cut, and the three front buttons were placed closer together. The lapels were often large and pointed or curved. The flapped pockets were at hip level and ticket pockets could be on the inside of the jacket or set in an outside pocket. Double-breasted jackets usually had four to six buttons.

Light belted overcoat with patch pockets, c. 1936

The lady on the left is in a pleated dress of multi-coloured silk material with puffed sleeves and the bodice mounted and gathered onto a yoked waist. The front and back of the skirt are pleated. The gentleman is in a bowler hat and single-breasted lounge suit with wide, pointed lapels. On the right the parlourmaid is in the uniform of the period, c. 1936-39

In the 1930s jackets became fuller fitting around the chest, but closer fitting over the hips, and they had square shoulders. The lapels were soft rolling.

All jackets had long straight sleeves slightly shorter than the shirt sleeves so that about 1cm of the shirt cuffs protruded. This was deliberate, to show that gentlemen did no manual work and therefore there was no danger of the white cuffs interfering with easy movement and getting soiled.

Double-breasted evening waistcoat, c. 1933

WAISTCOATS

Waistcoat fronts were made either in materials to match the rest of the suit or jacket or in contrast, whilst the backs were of a cheaper lining material, either of silk or cotton and silk mixtures. The fronts were lined; in winter the lining was often of flannel or wool. At the back there was a strap and buckle made to be adjusted at the waist. The metal buckles were often oblong or oval in shape.

Double-breasted waistcoats were not as fashionable as the single-breasted type, although about 1923 there was a short revival of the double-breasted variety with collar and lapels. If the fastening was high the lapels were often low and rolling. Double-breasted waistcoats mainly had square cut fronts, but could have the points which were usually reserved for the single-breasted styles. There were usually three to four buttons on either side, whilst single-breasted waistcoats had more, usually up to about six. The bottom button was always left open.

In 1939, just before the Second World War, waistcoats were left off in the summer.

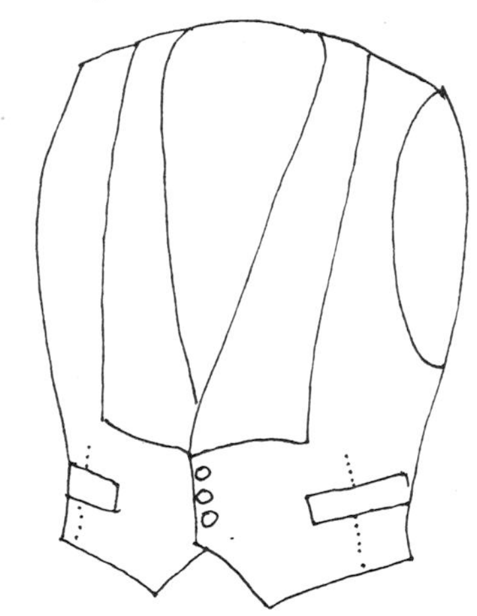

Single-breasted evening waistcoat, c. 1933

LEGWEAR

Just after the First World War trousers were narrower at the base than at the knees. From 1924 trouser legs became wider until by 1925 they were really baggy. These were known as Oxford bags, being first popularised by the undergraduates of Oxford. They reached a maximum width of about 60cm whereas legs had previously been only around 40cm wide. By about 1926 the extreme fashion of Oxford bags had subsided, but trousers remained wider in cut, with a better fit, and had two pleats in the waistband.

Trousers also became longer as their width increased; they were made to fall just over the instep.

From the mid-1920s trousers were usually striped when worn with morning or frock coats as well as black lounge

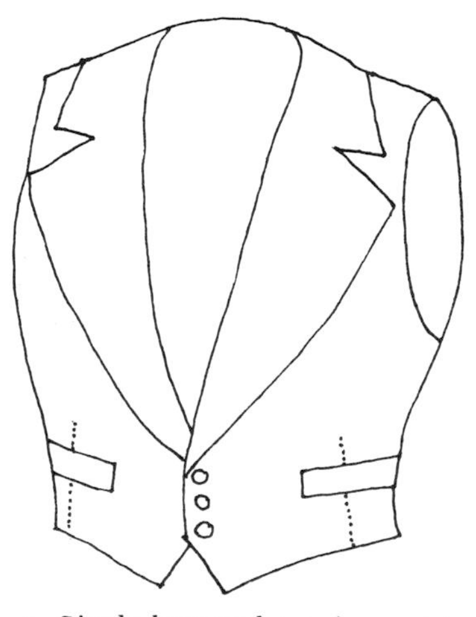

Single-breasted evening waistcoat, c. 1933

jackets and waistcoats. Trousers worn with double-breasted lounge jackets had permanently pressed turn-ups.

About 1922 flannel trousers were popular. At the waist they were made level all round, with side straps and loops to tighten them, instead of brace buttons. If necessary, belts and buckles were also employed.

Instead of the usual buttons and fly-front closure, zip fasteners were beginning to make an appearance, but still with the hook and bar at the waistline. Sometimes the waistband was made slightly longer on the left to protrude beyond the fly and was closed with a metal hook to a flat bar on the opposite side of the waistband. Straps either at the back or one each side were also attached and could be tightened with a button – the button being on the waist-band itself and the buttonhole on the loose strap. Belt loops on the waistband were also popular and a belt of self material or of leather could be threaded through.

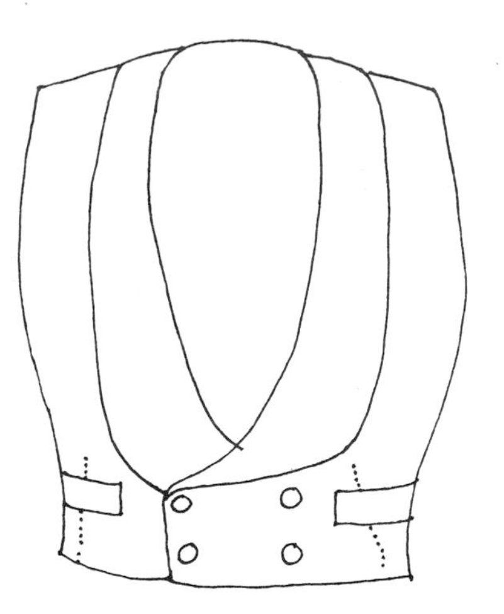

Double-breasted evening waist-coat, c. 1933

NECKWEAR

Starched white linen collars were popular. Wing collars, which were really stand collars with the front points bent down, were worn with evening dress. By about 1930 wing collars were only worn on formal occasions and with evening attire, and soft stand-fall collars were worn for dinner suits.

Both separate and attached soft collars were also worn. Soft double collars, the stand-fall type, were very popular. They were either in white or matched a coloured or patterned shirt. The separate collars were held in place by two button-holed tabs which were attached to a stand at the front, beneath a tie. Celluloid stiffeners were inserted between a double piece of material at the points of the collars. Stiff linen stand-fall collars were also quite fashionable. The collar points could vary in length, but they became longer from about 1935. There were various kinds of ties, bow ties being very popular when worn with wing collars. For evening wear, with dress suits, white piqué bow ties were worn, whilst with a dinner jacket, black silk was more usual. For day wear bow ties were mainly made of silk.

Long ties, known as four-in-hands, were the most usual style. The edges of the ties were horizontal with the top and bottom of the knot, and the ends could be squared or pointed.

Ties in school, club and regimental colours all gained in favour and were worn by many from the late 1920s.

Light summer coat with fly fastening and flapped pockets, c. 1920

OUTDOOR WEAR

Chesterfield coats remained fashionable throughout the period. They were probably the most popular coat worn. By about 1923 the Chesterfield was generally double breasted and had four to six buttons, a velvet collar and rolled lapels, and three outside pockets. It was sometimes fitted at the waist and had darts at the breast to give a good shape. By about 1926 neither the single- nor the double-breasted Chesterfield had a velvet collar any more, and the length was shortened to just below the knee to calf length. By 1935 the length was medium. The single-breasted Chesterfield often had a fly-front closure.

Ulster coats, not so modish, were worn mainly for travelling and country wear and were made in a warmer and heavier material than ordinary town coats. They were a looser fit, but could have a belt or a half belt. Capes or hoods were occasionally seen on them. About 1925 double-breasted Ulsters had belts and also either patch or inset pockets. From about 1930 fawn-coloured thick fleecy materials were popular. These thick woolly coats were also known as 'Teddy bear' coats. They were very popular as motoring coats but by 1939 became less fashionable.

Raglan coats, long and full with slits at the sides for the hands to reach the trouser pockets and vertical pockets, were fly fronted. The sleeves were cut with the seam from underarm, back and front, to the neckline. Raglans were often single breasted and could have patch pockets.

Another style of coat known as a *Newbury* was fly fronted with a velvet collar, a half belt and an inverted pleat at the back.

Raincoats of rubberised cotton were popular. Mackintoshes with belts, made of a lightweight material, were made to fold up so small that they could be carried in a pocket.

Short *Covert* coats, cut with raglan sleeves, were also used as showerproof coats. They were fly fronted and single breasted.

Raglan-sleeve style overcoat with slit pockets, c. 1939

FORMAL WEAR

For evening wear it was still necessary to wear tail coats for dinner dances in the early 1920s, although this habit was soon relaxed.

Dress coats were double breasted with cut-away fronts which sloped back increasingly in the early 1920s until they just covered the waistcoat. The tails, which had been knee length, also became slightly shorter. The coats became quite short waisted with inside breast pockets and pockets in the tails. The collar and rolling lapels were generally faced in silk. By the 1930s the shoulders had become square and the back wider. Lapels became larger and more prominent, and the tails reached to below the knees. About 1935 midnight blue was thought to give a darker appearance than black in artificial light, so this became a very modish colour.

Dinner jackets, which were at first fairly long, gradually became shorter, like the lounge jackets, until in the early 1920s they just covered the seat of the trousers. They were single breasted and worn open with sometimes just a link button at the waist. About 1925 roll collars and pointed lapels were worn and outside pockets were first seen. Jack Buchanan, a famous musical comedy star, popularised double-breasted dinner jacket styles, which became more fashionable than the single-breasted type in the 1930s. They had four buttons and the pockets were jetted or piped. The rolled lapels were higher than previously.

Trench coat style in gabardine, c. 1937

Waistcoats worn with tailcoats were mainly in white. The fronts were pointed with the single-breasted styles whilst double-breasted ones had the base square cut. Both types could have rolled collars with continuous lapels and two pockets. Double-breasted waistcoats had four to six buttons and the single-breasted only three to four. If three, these might be arranged as an inverted triangle.

Until about 1925, white waistcoats were worn with dinner jackets, but after that black became the acceptable colour.

About 1930 evening waistcoats could be backless, the fronts being joined at the collar and with a strap and buckle at the back, about waist level.

Trousers worn with evening wear followed the styles of day trousers, but were always without turn-ups. They were either of black or midnight blue to match the jackets with which they were worn. In the late 1920s and 1930s the outside seam was braided, one row of braid when worn with a dinner jacket and two with a dress coat.

Formal dress for weddings had been almost dropped during the First World War and just after that the usual dress for both groom and guests consisted of morning coat, black or striped waistcoat and striped trousers. Bow or long ties were worn with a wing collar. White spats and gloves with a walking stick and a silk top hat finished the ensemble. In the mid-1920s wedding attire became less formal and it was permitted to wear a lounge jacket with striped trousers and spats; gloves and sticks became unfashionable. Frock coats with lighter coloured waistcoats were worn mainly by older men. It was fashionable throughout the period to wear a white flower, usually a carnation, in the lapel buttonhole and a white handkerchief in the breast pocket.

For funerals, although frock or mourning coats were still occasionally seen, by the 1930s dark suits and black ties were the accepted wear. The mourning period was much reduced and it was usual to wear just a black tie and an armband.

Dress suits and white cotton gloves were worn for dancing out.

Evening dress coats and breeches were worn at Court after the war, but in 1937 new regulations came into force, in which it was laid down that the dress coat was to be worn with trousers which had to have gold lace braid down the outside side seam.

Dinner jacket suit with cummerbund, c. 1934

INFORMAL AND SPORTS WEAR

Smoking jackets, the popular colours being brown or maroon silk or velvet, were either single or double breasted. They were ornamented with frogging and with cord around the edges, and in the 1930s the edges could be bound in silk. Silk facings were often combined with quilting on the roll collars and cuffs. Smoking jackets could be worn with both day and evening trousers.

Tweed jackets and grey flannel trousers were very popular for informal occasions. The sports jackets were similar to the single-breasted lounge jackets with notched lapels. They could have a back vent and three buttons and patch pockets or they could be without the slit and have two ordinary pockets.

Blazers were popular in the summer, either single or double breasted. The usual colour was navy blue with gilt or brass buttons. The top breast patch pocket could carry the badge of a club or regiment.

Just around 1939 yoked sports jackets, similar to Norfolk jackets with a half belt behind and sometimes a pleated back, again became fashionable.

Sleeveless knitted *pullovers* with V-shaped necklines became popular. The neckband and hem could be in a contrasting colour or perhaps the club colours. Slip-on sweaters with turtle necks or high turned-over collars were

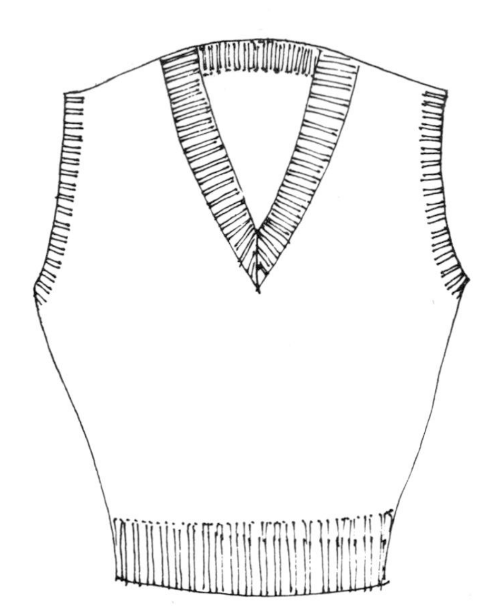

Sleeveless pullover, c. 1932

Plus fours golfing attire, c. 1928

also popular. Knitted waistcoats with various designs were also worn, but were replaced in the 1920s by sleeveless pullovers which were shorter than sweaters. Cardigans were knitted and were made like long close-fitting jackets with roll collars. For golfing, cardigans and stockings were knitted to match.

For hunting, red and black frock coats with buckskin breeches and top boots were worn with a top hat until about 1925. By about 1926 the frock coats were made in a single-breasted style, and swallowtail coats as well as full-skirted morning coats were also worn. For shooting, the fashion did not change from before the war: tweed jackets with breeches or plus fours, stockings, boots and gaiters and helmet shaped hats with earflaps were acceptable wear. *Hacking jackets*, which were lounge jackets in a long full-skirted style with a centre vent and two side slits, were worn for riding. Jodhpurs began to replace the cavalry twill breeches in the 1920s. Hard hats or reinforced riding caps were essential, and string gloves fashionable.

Cricket outfits did not alter very much; they still consisted of white flannel trousers and shirts with white boots. White sweaters and blazers with the club badge were also worn.

Tennis wear was similar to that for cricket, but in the 1930s white shorts gradually replaced the long white trousers.

Footballers generally wore woollen jerseys or cotton shirts with knee-length shorts which in the 1930s gradually became shorter.

For golf, sports jackets and Norfolk jackets with baggy knickerbockers or trousers were worn in the early 1920s. By about 1925 plus fours, jackets and Fair Isle pullovers had become popular. Soft felt hats became more fashionable than the older type of close-fitting peaked caps. In the early 1930s plus fours were replaced by trousers, and shirts with a collar and tie were worn with pullovers. Waist-length golf jackets of waterproofed material or suede had close fitting waists and were tight at the wrists, both waist and wrist being usually of a knitted material. Fastening was with buttons or a zip, usually to one side to prevent pouching in the front.

For cycling, except for enthusiasts who still wore knickerbockers, trousers were worn, with cycle clips to prevent the bottoms getting caught in the cycle chain.

At the seaside flannel trousers, usually in white, were the

normal attire, together with a shirt, tie and a blazer. Straw or felt hats were also worn. Light-coloured linen suits were also popular and in the 1930s open necked shirts without ties were worn with shorts.

Bathing costumes, mainly made of cotton, were worn in the 1920s and were often in two parts, bathing trunks and a top, some with overskirts, in the late 1920s. They were mainly in black or navy blue. Until the mid-1930s the back of the bathing costume could be cut in a Y shape, with shoulder straps and a very narrow back piece. From about 1935 bathing trunks became more popular than the previous suits.

Blue *Reefer* suits, Reefer jackets with white trousers, or single-breasted white suits were the general wear for yachting, with peaked caps and white canvas shoes. In inclement weather yachting equipment included oilskins.

Leather coats were popular for motoring, but special clothes were worn less as it became more general and less of a sport.

For skiing in the late 1920s waterproofed breeches with oiled stockings and gloves with thick woollen sweaters, matching caps and scarves were worn.

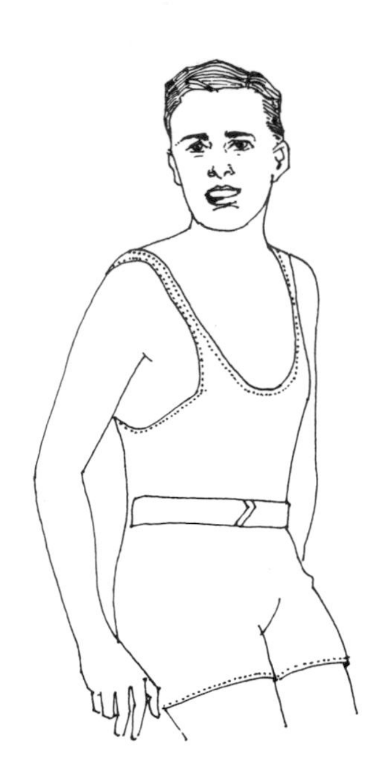

Swim or sunsuit with a belt at the waist, c. 1929

FOOTWEAR

Shoes became pointed and were generally made of brown calfskin or white buckskin with brown toecaps. Until about 1925 shoes remained fairly high. Boots were sometimes made with cloth tops. Some boots were still fastened with buttoning, whilst others were laced, with eyelets at the bottom and through hooks from the ankles up. In summer boots and shoes were often made of either canvas or buckskin and could be trimmed with brown, tan or black, being the typical 'co-respondent' shoes of the 1920s.

Smart young men often wore grey or white gloves to match their kid or felt-topped spats (which were occasionally also worn by women).

A style of polished calf leather shoe in tan, or 'yellow' as it was sometimes called, had deep square toes known as *American toes* or *Bulldogs* and became very popular. This style was machine made.

Broguing was popular for both sports and ordinary shoes. From about 1918 brogues were worn mainly informally with flannel suits. They were made fashionable by the Prince of Wales, later Edward VIII, who was very fond of

Golf shoe, c. 1922

Derby boot in kid leather, c. 1924

fringed tongues. In the 1930s brogues became heavier in style and were mainly worn for walking in the country.

For dancing and evening wear *pumps* were popular. These were soft flexible shoes, low cut in the front with a flat grosgrain bow decoration, and were often made of patent leather.

Another very popular fashion was the *Oxford type shoe* made in patent leather with the laces of a military braid. About 1918-20, younger men often wore the Oxford type shoe with a plain, almost pointed toecap and four-holed lace fastening. These were worn mainly with the long coats and wide trousers of the time.

The older men of the same period generally wore a type of half boot which had slightly rounded toes with cloth or suede tops and either leather or patent vamps. These boots were close fitting and were fastened with buttons.

Crêpe or rubber soles were increasingly used about 1921, especially for footwear worn in the country or for sports.

Sandals and sports shoes became popular wear: for sports, tan and white shoes were still fashionable and for the beach canvas plimsolls or sand shoes with rubber soles were worn.

In wet weather Wellington boots were worn, or galoshes, both made of rubber. The galoshes were a type of overshoe which were slipped over ordinary walking shoes.

Men's shoes generally developed a new freedom in both design and types of leather used, with suede becoming fashionable in the 1930s. By about 1938 shoe making and design had reached a high standard. Brown or black laced shoes of leather were very popular. *Monk's shoes*, popular in the 1930s, were sometimes of suede and had high tongues with a strap and buckle fastening. Boots declined in popularity, being mainly worn by the older men, or for country wear.

Socks could be coloured and striped or with patterns and clocks. They were held up with suspenders and reached mid-calf. For wear with knickerbockers, socks were made longer, to knee length, and held up by elasticated garters over which the tops were turned. These tops could sometimes be quite decorative. The advent of trouser turn-ups also encouraged the wearing of brightly coloured socks.

Two-tone or co-respondent leather shoes for casual and leisure wear, usually black or brown and white, c. 1938

Hand-sewn shoe in box calf, c. 1927

HAIRSTYLES

Hair was usually worn quite short with short back and sides and this remained the fashion generally throughout the period.

Man's hairstyle, c. 1925

The singeing of hair that was brittle or fine and sparse was recommended for stronger growth as this sealed the ends of the hair, thus retaining the natural oils necessary for thicker hair.

In the 1920s Rudolph Valentino, the famous film actor who wore his hair flat and plastered down, made this a very popular fashion. Also in vogue was waved hair, Marcel waving becoming the mode around 1922.

About 1923, short haircuts worn by the army influenced civilians, so that a short back and sides, but with sideburns, was worn by the majority. Also about 1923, side whiskers became fashionable, although not as pronounced as in the Victorian era. By the 1920s beards were less popular and were worn mainly only by the artistic and eccentric gentlemen.

Hair pieces and toupees were made to match hair colours and were worn extensively by balding men.

The moustache gradually declined in popularity in the 1930s. To give a moustache a natural appearance, it was usually curled with an iron or rolled on paper, and then combed out.

Centre partings with front waves remained popular throughout the period. The Pompadour – or raised hair in the front – was popular until about 1930. In the early 1930s hair was smoothed down with hair oil and brushed straight back from the forehead, being slightly raised in the front. One style was to brush the side hair towards the back to form a blunt point.

In the late 1930s, the most characteristic feature of hairstyles was the total lack of parting whatsoever; the hair was cut in such a way that the contour of the head was apparent. Just before the Second World War, in 1939, it was stylish to have hair brushed at the temples to form slightly raised wings either side.

About 1934 permanent waving for men became acceptable, and about 1935 beards and moustaches became the mode again. Beards were similar in style to those of 1918.

HEADWEAR

Hats were less popular after the First World War, due possibly to the fact that headwear had been compulsory with uniform. Another contributing factor was the increased use of the motor car. After the war the great variety in both hats and caps decreased.

Man's hairstyle, c. 1929

Man's hairstyle, c. 1934

Man's hairstyle, c. 1935

Boater, c. 1921

Silk top hat, c. 1921

Soft trilby-type hat with brim turned down all round, c. 1927

Small-brimmed bowler hat, c. 1935

Homburg-style hat, c. 1936

Top hats, except for formal occasions, were seldom worn. *Boaters* and *panama hats* were also seldom seen, boaters only being worn informally in the summer and by schoolboys.

Trilby hats, similar to Homburgs, but of a softer felt or velour, became almost a civilian uniform. They were worn by all kinds of professional people such as detectives, service officers and insurance brokers. The turned-up brims were bound in silk and the tops indented in the crown from the front to the back. Soft caps and other soft felt hats with the brims not bound with silk were increasingly worn. They were also much worn in the country.

Bowler hats were worn at race meetings as well as for city wear, where they were sometimes known as 'business' hats, but in the 1930s both bowlers and Homburgs were worn less, especially the Homburg which was replaced by a black trilby which became known as an Anthony Eden hat after Sir Anthony Eden, the politician. These hard trilby Eden hats were worn particularly on formal and business occasions with sombre suits or black jackets and black or grey and white striped trousers. With lounge suits the trilby hats were generally in grey or fawn and could be soft.

An adaptable soft felt hat in the trilby style became popular for both town and country wear. This had a small brim, sometimes bound with silk, which could be turned down front and back according to taste. In the early 1930s these were sometimes called *snap brim* or *curl brim* hats. By the mid-1930s the dent in the crown instead of being front to back, became rounded and the hats were then known as *pork pie* hats.

Formal hat styles altered very little after the First World War. Top hats, with the sides slightly concave, were mainly worn for weddings and race meetings, made in a grey cloth. Black top hats were rarely seen except with evening wear and occasionally with morning coats.

BEAUTY AIDS

Mud packs were used by men as well as women to smooth the skin and draw out blemishes. Moustache cups were made with a chin bridge across the inside of the cup to support the moustache and prevent it from getting wet when drinking, thus preserving the shape. After-shave creams and powders became popular in the late 1920s to 30s and were excused as being soothing to chapped skin.

ACCESSORIES

Gloves were always worn for town wear – of chamois or kid or of cloth. In the 1920s fastening at the wrists was generally with one button. In the 1930s gloves were less popular and were worn mainly for driving. These gloves were often of string or leather.

For evening wear *scarves* were generally of woven silk or a fine wool. For day wear they could be plain or in coloured designs. Club colours were also much worn. Fringed ends were quite usual.

Spats, which covered the tops of shoes and ankles and buttoned on the outside, were held in place under the shoe with a strap and buckle. Grey was one of the most popular colours, but white was worn at weddings. Spats were generally made of a strong cotton or canvas. By 1939 they had almost completely gone out of fashion.

Gaiters, which were like long spats, reaching up the calf, were worn for outdoor sports such as golf and shooting.

Walking sticks declined in popularity in the 1920s. Canes, when carried, often had recesses to hold small items such as cigarettes, pipes, etc. The handles could be straight or crooked with silver bands and tips.

Umbrellas were carried and were tightly furled. At the start of the 1920s crook handles were popular, but gradually cane handles with joints, as well as leather covered handles, also became fashionable.

Silk, linen and cotton *handkerchiefs* were usually white but could have coloured borders. Sometimes the wearer's initial was embroidered in one corner. It was fashionable to wear a handkerchief in the outside breast pocket with a small part showing.

Wrist watches, first worn before the First World War, with leather straps, became universal wear from the 1920s. They were either square or oblong. Pocket watches were eventually only worn for dress wear, but with the decline of dress coats, wrist watches were the usual wear.

Tie pins could be of the stick or clip variety. They were generally of gold or silver and could have a precious jewel at the head for ornamentation. In the mid-1920s tie pins were less frequently used but a safety pin type could be worn to hold long ties in place. Gold safety pins were sometimes worn either side of stiff collars to hold them in place in the early 1920s, and gold clips were used under stiff collars. With the advent of semi-stiff collars, the safety pins were no longer required.

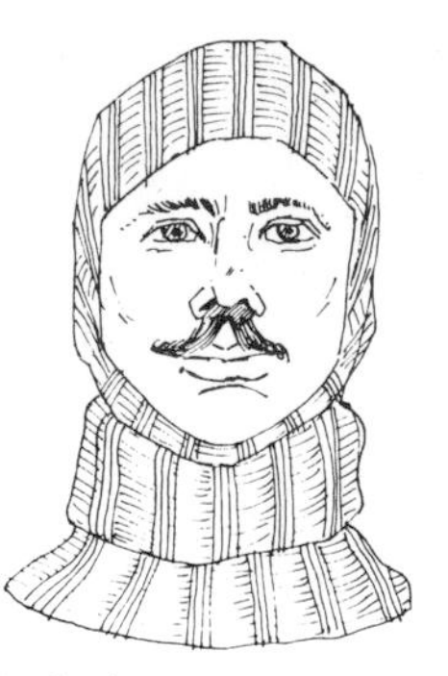

Balaclava or plain knitted helmet, early 1920s

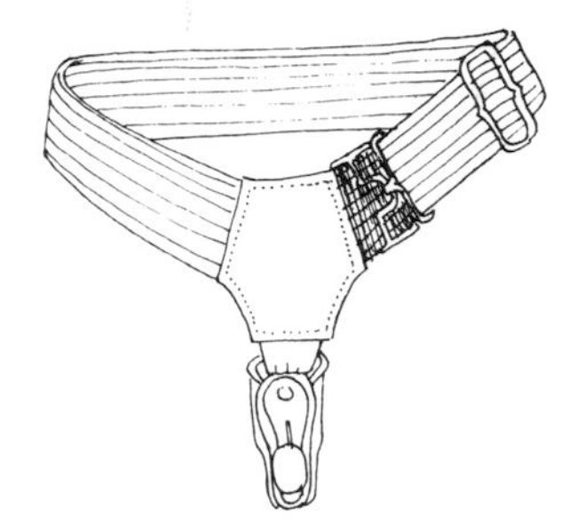

Suspender worn around the calf to hold up sock, c. 1930

Felt trilby hat, c. 1938

Soft, snap brim trilby-style hat, c. 1939

Cuff links were popular, but when cuff buttons became more commonly used the need for cuff links decreased, although for evening wear they were still frequently used and made to match collar studs and waistcoat buttons. A popular style was gold based with a mother-of-pearl covering.

Signet rings were popular throughout the period. They were mainly in gold with semi-precious stones.

The lady is in a dance dress with godets and an uneven hemline. The gentleman is in evening dress with tails, c. 1927

Women

Ankle-length wrap-over style coat with belt and fringe-decorated cuffs, worn with large brimmed hat with chiffon hatband and flower trimming, c. 1921

With the levelling of classes and the emancipation of women, clothes reflected a new freedom. Skirts became shorter and clothes took on a more relaxed look, becoming looser. Cutting fabrics on the bias made materials more pliable and easier to drape.

By about 1918 skirts, which were calf length, became straighter and remained so until about 1922 when they again became longer, almost reaching the ankles. Once they again became shorter they continued to do so until they revealed the knees in about 1925-27, this being the shortest style so far in the history of fashion.

From about 1910 to 1922 the waistline, at about the natural level, was emphasised by a belt or sash, but after that period a flatter, straighter silhouette became popular. Waistlines disappeared, and women tried to flatten thier bust. The new shape meant that the dress was straight from the shoulder to the hemline, with the bodice being joined low, at hip level. Another style was a straight skirt worn with a long blouse, not tucked in, or else a hip length *jumper* of a knitted material; this was also an innovation. Even tailored suits followed the new tubular line with straight cut jackets. By about 1927 skirts were at their shortest. Hairstyles became extremely short and often severe, the shortest being the Eton crop style of 1927. Cloche hats were worn with these styles.

About 1929 hemlines were lowered and by about 1931 they again reached calf length. The new mode was for a long slender appearance, being softer than previously. Skirts were either gored or flared and cut on the cross, made so

1 *On the left is a lady in a day dress made of silk to a modern design with flounces at the back and sides. c.1932.*

The lady in the centre is wearing a three-quarter length fashionable top coat with a deep shawl collar and straight sleeves. The waist and side panels are fringed. A large-brimmed felt hat is worn. c.1919.

The other lady is in an evening dress of 'twenties fashion. The straight shapeless dress was arranged in tiers and made in lace. An ostrich feather fan was carried. The bob style haircut was popular. c.1925.

2 *The gentleman is wearing a light single-breasted lounge suit with a two button fastening. The single-breasted waistcoat is cut high with a V opening. The trousers were becoming wider, the forerunners of the Oxford bags. He is wearing a trilby hat. c.1923.*

In the centre is a lady in a tailor-made skirt with a short belted jacket. The cuffs of the blouse beneath are turned back over the jacket sleeve. She is wearing a beret. c.1937.

The lady on the right is wearing the shapeless dress of the early 1920s, with a large bowed sash low on the waistline. The large picture hat was decorated with a garland of flowers. c.1921.

The lady on the left is in an ankle-length fur-trimmed velvet evening ensemble and the lady on the right in a day dress with tabard type overtunic, c. 1922

that they clung down as far as the hips and then flared out, with the waistline once more in the normal position, belts and sashes being worn.

In the 1930s more romantic styles emerged with wider shoulders and puffed sleeves. Dresses became more flowing and softer hairstyles with waves and ringlets were worn. Evening dresses were backless and reached the ground. By the mid-1930s the skirts could also have inverted pleats and the tailored jackets usually had wide lapels and one to three buttons for fastening. From about 1937 when skirts gradually became shorter, hats became much more decorative. Inset sleeves were often puffed or given the impression of widened shoulders with padding.

Coats could be loose, of the swagger type or belted, and might have either set-in or raglan style sleeves.

DAY DRESSES

Dresses were generally made in one piece or the bodice and skirt could be joined at the waistline. Until the early 1920s bodices were usually lined, and if the dresses were made of a light material the skirts could also be lined or worn with an underskirt. One piece dresses, which gave a straighter line, became fashionable as did frocks that buttoned down the front to the waist. The latter could be single or double breasted with a belt and buckle or sash to cover the join of bodice and skirt. The skirt might be pleated or flared and the collar high and closed or turned down flat with revers. These frocks could resemble a tailor-made dress and were worn in the summer made up in lightweight materials and in the winter made of wool.

Two piece dresses similar to jumper dresses sometimes had a short sleeveless overdress that could be worn over a skirt, with shoulder straps hidden beneath the top. Very often a sash was also worn. Accordion pleats were also fashionable for skirts that were worn with jumpers.

For afternoon wear, hip length *overtunics*, sometimes open at the sides, could be removed when the dresses were worn for afternoon dances. The necklines were fairly low, and, if square, without collars. Rounded or V-shaped décolletages often had the popular sailor collars. Some afternoon dresses, instead of overtunics, had waistcoats which could be in contrasting material to the dress itself.

From the 1920s day dresses were mainly in one piece, joined at the waist. Two piece versions usually consisted of

Calf-length dress with three-quarter length matching coat worn with large brimmed hat with feather decoration, c. 1919

Short-sleeved day dress with scalloped bodice attached to the pleated skirt with buttoning, worn with large straw picture hat, c. 1920

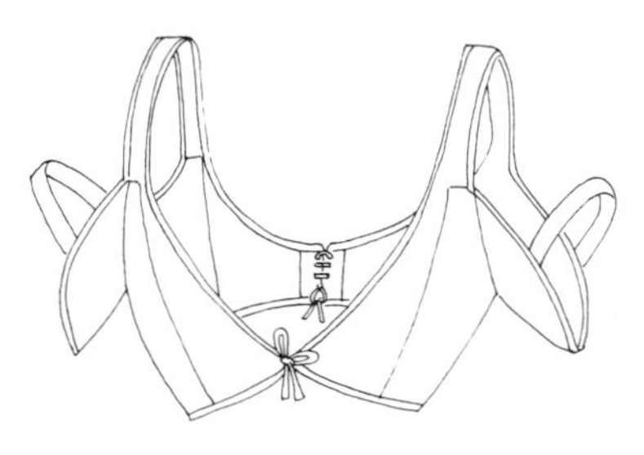

Dress shield, c. 1925-26

a skirt and blouse or jumper. In the 1920s the waistlines were lowered and skirts became slightly longer and wider. *Overskirts* with scalloped trimmings or points at the hemline were popular, as were tunics which could be panelled or made to resemble aprons. The skirts of the dresses were often accordion pleated. For afternoon wear fur trimmings and lace insertions were also fashionable.

Around 1924 the tunic styles became narrower with a straighter silhouette and shorter skirts. The tunics could be long to the knees, like a long straight bodice, and worn over a sheath skirt. By 1925 the waist join, which had gradually been lowered, had reached the hips and was indicated by a belt. To give more width to the straighter skirts, gores or godets could be inserted. Scalloped hemlines were often decorated with ruching or braid which followed the scalloped edge.

During the late 1920s skirt hems hung about 50cm to 45cm from the ground. Overskirts were made in pleating, with scarf effects with points hanging down like petals, or panels and even ruffles.

By about 1928 skirts reached knee level again and were often yoked from the waist to the hips and then allowed to flare out. By the end of the 1920s the waistline had begun to rise to its natural level again and skirts became a little longer once more, until in the early 1930s day dresses were again below knee level whilst afternoon dresses could be as much as 20cm below the knees. The skirts were close fitting to the hips and then flared out, sometimes being made in two or more layers.

Barrel shaped dresses reminiscent of the hobble skirts were also worn as teagowns, although teagowns as such gradually declined in usage. They were usually ankle length with wide Magyar sleeves. The dresses were rather shapeless and might have a detachable train. They could also be yoked and pleated, or decorated with frills. Sometimes a plaited girdle was also worn. Afternoon dresses, often with uneven hemlines, sometimes had deep fringe trimmings as well as lace.

By 1927 skirts were often cut on the bias or in a circular shape, so that they were very flared. Side decorations were quite the mode and were usually on the left side. They consisted of large bows, flounces, gathered panels, etc. and were sometimes sewn to the skirt on a slant. Pleating, however, was mainly confined to one side. Matching coats, either the same length or slightly shorter than the dresses themselves, were also fashionable at this time.

Dress necklines could have almost any shape including a boat shape. High closed collars were worn around 1921 and low V necks were also in the mode, worn with a fill-in, or a scarf or neckerchief so tied that the knot was at the point of the V. Round necklines had Peter Pan collars or larger flat collars which could have pointed ends. Medici style collars were still occasionally seen in the early 1920s. Revers were also popular.

The bodices themselves were often enhanced with embroidery and other decoration. Yoked bodices were fashionable around 1927 when the waistlines again became more prominent. At the end of the 1920s the bodice was often made with a blouse effect, thus slightly accentuating the bosom again. More drapery on the bodice as well as the skirts became apparent, but often only on one side. Cape back effects also became popular.

Most sleeves were at first long and tight but by 1926 bell shaped sleeves and shorter sleeves with cuffs were also worn. Dresses could be sleeveless when worn for afternoon wear or in the summertime. By this time a softer look with puffed sleeves and cuffs at the wrists was also popular.

In the 1930s day dresses made in one piece were of various types, some with overtunics, boleros or matching coats. *Pinafore* dresses became the mode from about 1931. They were made without sleeves, with a button closure at the back, and were usually worn over blouses or jumpers or could be worn on their own in the summer as a casual dress.

Princess styles always remained popular as did *shirt dresses* which, although made in one, had the bodice like a shirt with collar and revers, buttoning down the front to the waist seam.

In the early 1930s dresses hung about 30cm from the ground, whilst afternoon dresses were longer and as the 30s advanced both day and evening dresses became slightly longer. From the beginning of the 1930s until the mid-30s waistlines were slightly raised. The skirts could be either straight or cut on a slight bias and might be on a yoke.

Tunic frocks, which were fairly straight, as well as overtunics worn over close-fitting dresses were still worn in the late 1930s.

Dress skirts had hip yokes or could fall in a V or have an

Short knee-length waistless and sleeveless dress worn with deep cloche hat with turned-down brim, c. 1927

The lady on the left is in an elongated dress with a heart-shaped neckline and pouched bodice attached to a low waistline. The other two ladies are in dresses with boat-shaped necklines. The dresses are elongated, with the sleeves cut in one. The mid-calf skirts have low hip belts, c. 1923

The lady holding the dog on a lead is in a knee-length wrap-over style coat and a pull-on hat with floppy brim. The lady on the right is in a knitted jumper suit with a knee-length pleated skirt, c. 1928

upward curve or inverted V around the waistline. The skirts were fuller than previously, this effect being achieved with flares, pleats and tiers. Another style of skirt was an Austrian country style, known as a *dirndl*. This was made with straight pieces of material joined together and gathered at the waist with elastic. By 1938 day dresses with small waistlines and fully flared or gathered skirts were fashionable and hems were about 35cm off the ground. The waistlines were often pulled in by a wide belt. In 1939 it was the mode for these full skirts to have an apron in matching material added; this was often tied with a sash. Full skirts, achieved with pleating, circular cuts, flounces, tiers and even bows at the back were very popular, worn with tight fitting bodices which could have separate collars. These gave an effect of children's dresses.

Dress bodices in the 1930s had wide accentuated shoulders. The bodices could be basqued, and for afternoon dresses folds and drapery were still popular. Closure could be at the front or back, or diagonally to give an added interest to the design. Décolletages were in a variety of styles. V necklines with fill-ins were still popular, or the effect could be accomplished by having a cross-over front tied at the back or side with the girdle ends. Cape collars and cowl necklines were also still fashionable. In the period 1933-36 the wide severe shoulder line went out of fashion, but returned again later. During this time neckerchiefs, jabots, bows and frilly collars were all much in vogue.

Two-piece costume with hip-length jacket buttoned at the waist only, deep cuffs and matching deep collar, c. 1920

From 1936 yoked collars came into fashion and bosoms were accentuated by breast pockets, pleats and gathers. The skirts also supported this emphasis by inverted V shapes from the waist with the bodice gathered to the waistline.

Tunic or shift dresses, gathered at the waist with a sash or a belt, were full from the shoulders down, with gauging or smocking at neck and shoulders also being in the mode. They could be knee length or a little shorter. Some tunic dresses, if short, were worn over simple long-skirted frocks, and in winter could be fur trimmed.

Bodice sleeves varied in length, and some afternoon frocks could even be sleeveless in the early 1930s. From about 1931 *bishop* sleeves were popular and were very fashionable. Bell-shaped sleeves were worn from 1936 and 1937 saw sleeves full to the elbow and then tight fitting to the wrist. *Raglan* and *Magyar type* sleeves were also popular. Short sleeves could be caped or puffed, and towards the end of the 1930s fairly tight-fitting sleeves were in gathers or folds from the elbows down to the wrists. Shoulders were wide in the early 1930s, beginning to be sloped and softer in shape around 1934 when dropped shoulder seams, below shoulder level, could be seen. Padded shoulders were also fashionable from about 1936.

Loose jumper blouse, c. 1923

JUMPER SUITS AND DRESSES

Jumper dresses consisted of a skirt with a matching jacket or jumper that could be buttoned and basqued and belted. The two-piece dresses sometimes just had a skirt with a matching bolero and a contrasting blouse.

Jumper suits were generally made of lightweight or knitted materials. Pleated skirts were popular and sometimes the jumper was part of the skirt. In the 1920s jumpers reached the hips, but by the 1930s they had become shorter. The jumpers could have V necklines and the neck edges and border hems of the ensemble might be decorated. Matching hip-length sleeveless jackets, with ribbed hems to give a better fit, were often worn over the jumper suits.

COSTUMES AND TAILORED SUITS

Costumes and two-piece suits became more popular than in previous times. They were generally worn with a blouse or shirt.

Around 1930 three-piece suits became the mode. They consisted of skirt, jacket and overcoat and were often made of a tweed material, with the jacket short and tailored, falling over a belt. Very often the tailor-made suits were made by men's tailors.

The jackets in the 1920s were fairly straight and made similar to a man's lounge suit, although they could be basqued or have flounces so that the hips were accentuated. Pleats were also popular and if belts or half belts were worn, the waistline was further accentuated. Sailor collars were very fashionable and were made detachable; they often had long, hanging fronts. Some jackets were more cape-like and worn with waistcoats – one style known as 'batswing' had caped sleeves.

About 1921 the jackets were often long and straight with pointed lapels, the coats of knee length or three-quarter length. The collars could be high or of the sailor variety. Fastening was often with links. By about 1923 the waist-

Square-necked loose-fitting blouse, c. 1923

line was lowered with flounces on the hips, or the coat belt could be at hip level. Wrap-over styles were also popular with waistcoats worn beneath them. The jacket sleeves were often cuffed with buttons.

By about 1926 long jackets were worn over whole dresses. The suits could also be worn with matching overcoats which were often made of a warmer material for the winter. Jackets closed at the front with links, similar to men's dinner jackets, became fashionable.

Two-toned belted summer blouse with long sleeves, c. 1932

Until about 1936 suits could be of matching or contrasting colours and materials, jackets often being of a lighter colour than the skirts. Suede was popular for the jackets, whilst corduroy or cloth was used for the skirts. Matching hats were also worn with the ensemble from about 1934.

In the 1930s coat jackets were waisted and began to look quite masculine. They often had rounded ends and could have scarf collars, and be belted or basqued. Pointed lapels were also popular in the early part of this decade. The jackets became straighter and looser, similar to box coats. Waistcoats were often worn beneath. Until about 1930 the jacket sleeves were straight and tight, either full-length or ending just below the elbow. After this they became wider and were padded at the shoulders, but by 1934 they again became softer looking with sloping shoulders. *Reefer* type jackets were also worn and by about 1935 three-quarter length loose coat jackets became the mode. They were loose fitting and known as *swagger* or *jigger* coats.

Boleros, from about 1937, were worn with three-piece suits with a skirt and top coat or cape. Single-breasted jackets which had high necklines and wide lapels or collars were worn as well as collarless jackets with wide revers that buttoned only at the waist with one button. Fur and braid trimmings were fashionable throughout.

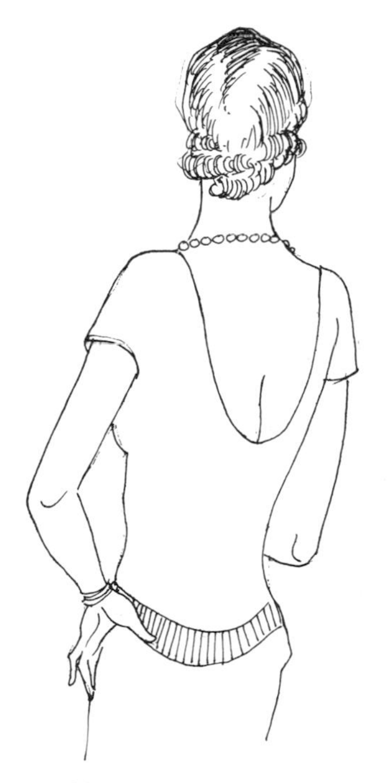

Backless summer blouse, c. 1932

A *jumper-waistcoat*, a kind of blouse worn over the skirt, was popular from about 1919. The borders were often embroidered or tasselled and the sleeves generally three-quarter length. Fur trimming was popular in the winter.

From about 1920 V necks with wide pointed collars were popular as well as collarless blouses. Cross-over styles were also much worn. Shirt blouses worn, mainly for sport, with suits were loose fitting in the early 1920s and generally fastened at the front.

Jumper blouses, known as jumpers, were a type of knitted coat, later known as cardigans or jerseys.

Blouses worn with suits were often tucked into the waistband of the skirt; they could be elasticated at the waist or have a drawstring. Longer styles could be worn outside the skirt and were sometimes similar to tunic blouses. They could also be belted. Long bell-shaped or *bishop* sleeves were popular early in the 1920s, and short sleeves or none at all were fashionable for summer wear. Necklines varied from V shaped to round with a scarf or tie knotted at the base of the opening. They could have high or stand-up collars. By about 1929 scarf collars were popular. They were collars where the front ends continued long enough to be tied into either a bow or knot in the front. By about 1930 blouses might have yokes of contrasting colours.

Skirts often had braces attached to hold them up. These braces could be made of the same material or in a patent leather. They could also be attached to artificial silk underbodices, similar to those worn by little girls. The straight skirts often had decorated stitched seams at front and back, and the narrower styles could have side pleats. Barrel shaped skirts, from 1918, became fashionable, probably because of shortages of material after the First World War. About 1919 suit skirts gradually became longer and could be pleated, either at the sides or all the way round.

The straight or panelled skirts of the 1920s could have hip yokes and side panels, and kilting – pleats at the back – was popular from about 1922 when skirts were about 20cm off the ground. Skirts were sometimes sewn on to a petersham ribbon band.

Wrap-over skirts, as well as a waterfall type, with drapery on one side, also became fashionable from 1924 when skirts rose to 30cm from ground level. Until this time patterned skirts were often worn with plain jacket or coat tops.

By about 1927 open pleats and knife pleats were popular and skirts rose yet again to be about 40cm from the ground, but by around 1930 they had again become a little longer, reaching about 35cm.

In the 1930s skirts often had pleats in groups, either at the front, back or side. Flared skirts were also worn. In the mid-1930s the front panels of skirts could be cut on the cross, whilst the rest was straight cut. Another fashion was for skirts flared only from the knees, or with inverted pleats. Box pleats were also popular. By about 1936 straight skirts, known as pencil skirts, were popular. Many skirts were cut on the cross to give a better fit.

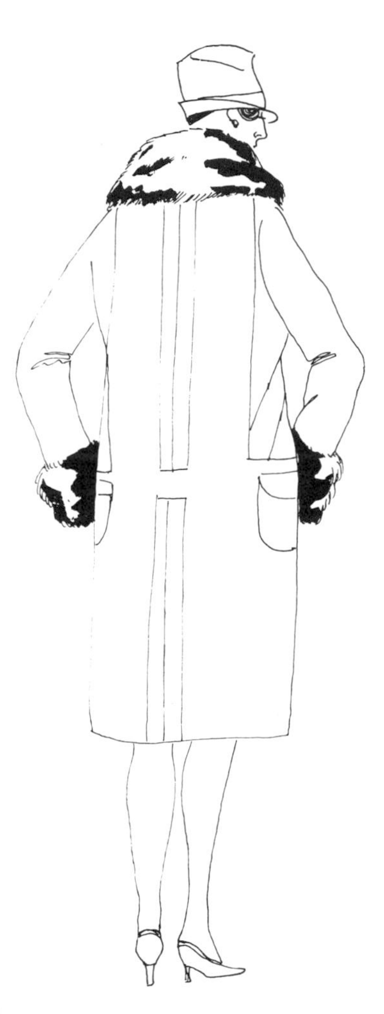

Loose-fitting coat with large fur collar and matching cuffs, worn with deep cloche hat with upturned brim at the back, c. 1926

The figure on the left is in a woollen dress and jacket which is three-quarter length. The skirt is pleated from the waist at the side. A cloche type hat and pochette style handbag complete the outfit. The background figure is in a belted coat with large pockets. The cloche hat has a turned-down brim, c. 1930

Many skirts worn with blouses had pockets at the sides or slit pockets and belts of the same material.

KNITWEAR

Jumpers were mainly worn with contrasting skirts, usually for country and informal day wear. They could also be worn with tailored suits instead of blouses in colder weather. Jumpers were loose fitting to waist or hip level, without a neck fastening, but were just slipped on over the head. They were generally of a knitted or crocheted wool or silk. The popularity of hand knitting and crocheting during the First World War encouraged the making of these jumpers and other knitted clothes such as dresses and cardigans. They were made in a variety of styles and could have patterns knitted or crocheted into the design. Knitwear could be belted or have ties at the sides. Necklines were V shaped, round or square, and sleeves could be of any length. Magyar sleeves were also popular.

Dresses and suits could be hand or machine knitted in wool or artificial silk. At first the shapes were fairly straight, the suit jackets quite long with a knitted tie belt or a leather belt around the waist.

Sleeveless jerseys and jumpers were often worn over blouses. Many jumpers and cardigans were made to match and worn with skirts and matching coats. These jumpers and cardigans were later known as twin sets and were often made in plain classical styles with rounded necklines and long raglan type sleeves.

Towards the end of the 1920s the jumpers and cardigans became longer, but in the early 1930s again became shorter when worn with matching coats and skirts. Fair Isle patterns were popular as well as horizontal stripes and criss-cross patterns. If the knitwear was fairly plain, the hems and neck edges were often in a contrasting colour. Wool became more popular for jumpers, etc. than knitted silks. V necks were as fashionable as high necklines with turned down collars. The fronts could also be made in a cross-over style with a chemisette fill-in. Cardigans could be sleeveless, worn like waistcoats. They could have low neck openings or be high with scarf collars as well as lapelled collars. Sometimes cardigans had pockets. In 1933 an elastic silk or velvet material was the mode for jumpers worn for semi-formal occasions.

In the mid-1930s ensembles consisting of jumper, skirt

Low V-necked décolletage filled in with a pleated chiffon front. The silk afternoon dress has a hemline of handkerchief points worn under a sleeveless matching silk coat, three-quarter length and trimmed at the neck with fur, c. 1928

and cardigan, all knitted, were sometimes teamed with matching knitted berets and handbags. The necklines could be made to drape, and if the jumpers or cardigans were fairly long they could also have a belt.

If jumpers and cardigans were very low necked, blouses were sometimes worn beneath. Large decorative buttons were fashionable and jumpers often had round or polo necks. Sleeves could be slightly puffed or of the kick-up variety. Decorative yokes and ribbing were also popular. Knitted suits with matching knitted coats often had collars, revers and flapped pockets.

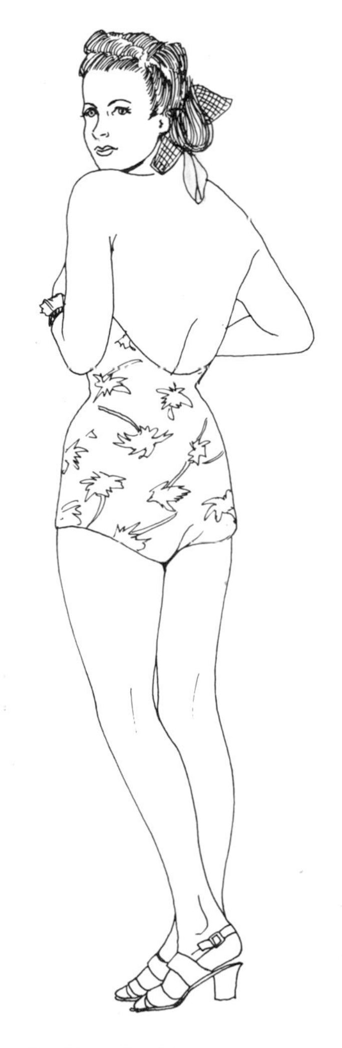
Backless bathing costume with halter neckline, c. 1938

TROUSERS

Trousers appeared in the 1920s, mainly for sport and evening leisure wear. The harem skirt or Turkish trousers worn for a brief while before the First World War did not become popular, although a dress made in one with an elasticated waist and split in two trouser legs was occasionally worn in the evenings. Pyjama suits made of heavy silks or brocades were worn mainly at home in the evenings.

For sportswear, trousers with turn-ups, similar to men's, were worn with a wide sash from about 1928 and pyjama like trousers could be worn with sleeveless boleros and a blouse for the beach. These were usually of a fine material such as crêpe de Chine.

In the 1930s trousers gained in popularity. They were worn increasingly at the seaside as well as for informal evening wear when they could be quite full and made to look like skirts.

Shorts were also being worn for sports – mainly in khaki for hiking and cycling, and reaching the knees. Divided skirts with inverted pleats were also popular. In the later 1930s tailored trouser suits, consisting of trousers and jackets, appeared in flannel and woollen materials. Trousers were generally fastened at the left side with a zip covered by a placket.

BLOUSES

Blouses were often short and worn over skirts and had short sleeves or cap sleeves. Criss-cross patterns as well as waistcoat effects were popular. Some short blouses buttoned up at the back. Drapery in the front as well as cowled necklines were much in vogue, with soft woollen or silky materials being used. Cross-over fronted blouses as well as tailored

The lady on the left is in a silk dress with a Zouave or Turkish hemline with a small train. Strings of beads were very popular. The lady on the right is in a draped teagown with a low-backed dēcolletage and strings of pearls and diamantē decorations, c. 1920-21

ones with collars and sometimes revers, and long tightish sleeves that had buttoned cuffs, were also fashionable. Yoked blouses or jabots and bows as well as frills were all popular.

Slim-fitting knee-length coat with thick bands of fur at the neck, down the front and cuffs, worn with soft cloche hat, c. 1926

EVENING WEAR

Evening dresses tended to be fairly tight fitting in the early 1920s whilst dresses worn for dancing were much fuller in the skirts. The overskirts were often of several layers of flounces ending at mid calf. Dance dresses could also have overtunics of a diaphanous material.

The longer evening dresses were still trained, but they were narrower, sometimes only the long ends of the sash forming a train. Narrow trains could also fall from the waist or shoulders at the back towards one side. The straight skirts often had draped overskirts and hems could be uneven. Drapery and ornamentation to one side was very popular as were long panels with pointed ends as well as petal shapes. Frills and sashes were much used to give added interest.

Many evening dresses became backless in the 1920s and, when sleeveless, the bodices were supported by either shoulder straps or halter necks. Beaded and sequined dresses were very popular.

In the early 1920s the waistline was lowered, but by about 1923 it was again slightly raised. A flatter look became fashionable around 1924 with overtunics. The natural waistline did not re-appear again until the end of the 1920s. Around 1925 skirts were sometimes shorter in the front than the back.

By the 1930s skirts had a more natural waist level and could be yoked. They were close fitting to the hips and then frilled. The skirts usually reached the ground.

Dance dresses often had godet pleating from the waist with flowers, bows and other decorations, mainly to one side, usually to the left. In the early 1930s dance dresses were shorter than evening dresses and reached only to the ankles. In the later 1930s they reached the calves and were very full, usually made of a light material such as tulle or lace.

In the early 1920s bodices were rather straight and shapeless with various décolletages, sometimes high but more usually low, with V or U necklines or in cross-over styles. Many dresses were sleeveless and also backless or very low backed. Diamanté shoulder straps or long wide transparent sleeves were also fashionable. The armholes were generally rather large.

Sashes could be worn over the shoulders with the ends tied at the hips, and then left to trail down the side giving a trained effect. Cape collars were fashionable and scarves could also be allowed to hang loosely behind.

From around 1926 pouched or bloused bodices with low décolletages were popular, the décolletage often lower at the back. One-sided effects were so popular that even necklines could be diagonally shaped.

By the end of the 1920s evening dresses were made to fit closer to the thighs and hems allowed to flare out. The décolletage at the back was sometimes so low that it almost reached the waist. In the 1930s it was also fashionable to have pouched backs. V-shaped or square-necked backs became the mode around 1933 and dresses with cape sleeves, capes and epaulettes and puffed sleeves were as popular as those without sleeves. The fronts of the bodices could be pleated over the bosom, with shirring beneath and between the breasts to give more emphasis to the shape of the body. Belts which were wide and in an inverted V at the front also helped to stress the shape. Towards the end of the 1930s heart shaped necklines became very popular, and halter necks as well as strapless bodices gained in favour. With extremely low backed dresses it was fashionable to wear a bolero or jacket which was sometimes of fur.

For dinner wear, a blouse and long pleated skirt was often worn.

Skirts in the 1930s were often cut on the cross so that they were close fitting to the knees from where they were allowed to flare out. Bustle effects were still sometimes achieved with the use of bows and ruching behind.

In the 1920s evening cloaks often had silk brocade linings and could have large fur collars. About 1924 capes were mainly cut in a circular shape and gathered to a fur collar. Coats were made in brocades to match evening wear, and in the mid-1920s had Oriental designs.

In the 1930s evening wraps were long to three-quarter length. They could be of velvets or brocades. The sleeves were often very wide and the wraps full and loose, fastening mainly from the neck only. Evening coats had tight-fitting bodices but very full skirts. With the fuller flared evening or dance skirts, short wraps or shawls were worn.

Trouser or *pyjama suits*, reflecting an Oriental influence.

Off the shoulder boat-shaped neckline; cape-sleeved evening dress in the tubular style with a three-tiered skirt, c. 1920

in velvet or metallic materials were very popular for a brief time in the 1920s.

In the early 1920s teagowns combined with the more formal afternoon or semi-evening dresses. These dresses were made of a very light and delicate material and were worn over satin or silk foundation slips or petticoats. The bodices could be cross-over in style or have V-shaped décolletages covered with jabots. The sleeves might end at the elbows, or if long, might be very frilly. Around the waist could be worn long sashes that were allowed to trail the ground at the back like a train. The skirts were sometimes pleated, or they could be panniered, and the hems could be scalloped.

During the 1930s a great many different leisure dresses were worn. The teagown or dinner frock was usually ankle length or just above, but if worn for afternoon teas or dances, it was usually shorter. The afternoon version could also be made with the bodice blouse and skirt separate.

Housegowns or housecoats, another variation of the teagown, were, in the late 1930s, made with long skirts, and could be made with wrap-over fronts, or buttoning down the front. Zips were also used occasionally. These coats were often made in a Princess line and mostly worn in the mornings and evenings for relaxation.

For cocktail wear, cocktail suits or pyjamas with wide trousers and tunic tops were very popular. These were made in velvets, satins or chiffon.

For cinema wear, in the mid-1930s, costumes were between calf and ankle length.

Coat frocks made like open-fronted dresses were less popular in the 1920s than they had been previously. They were often made to wrap over with a fastening to the side, usually the left. Patch pockets were often at the hips. Until about 1923 coat frocks were often cut in a Princess line, after which a waist seam was seen. The neckline could be rounded or square, and the collar could have long ends tied in the front. The coat frocks were made in heavy silks or cottons, but by the 1930s they were generally of tweed or coat materials and were sometimes tailored in design. At the waist they were often belted.

Evening dress with cross-over bodice and fairly full skirt, c. 1920

FORMAL WEAR

Wedding dresses were made in similar styles to evening dresses and were usually white. Although long dresses were mainly worn, shorter lengths as well as uneven hem lines were often seen in the 1920s. Sleeves were usually long. Veils of orange blossom wreaths were a popular form of head decoration. The head veils were sometimes so long that they replaced trains at the back. Juliet caps or coronets were also worn.

In the 1920s mourning periods became much shorter, and the wearing of mauve or violet was permitted as well as the usual black, although black armbands and black diamond shapes sewn to the sleeves of coats were also quite usual.

For maternity wear many skirts and dresses were made with adjustable waistlines, and loose smocks, either full length or worn over other dresses, were popular.

Court dress followed the styles of evening dress, but always with a train. In 1937 rules were laid down that Court dresses had to conform to. They had to be long with a train from the shoulders and a white veil with ostrich feathers was essential head wear. Except for mourning, when black feathers were permitted, they had to be white. Gloves, which also had to be worn, could be of any colour, as also could the Court dress. Bouquets and fans were allowed, although not a necessary part of the attire.

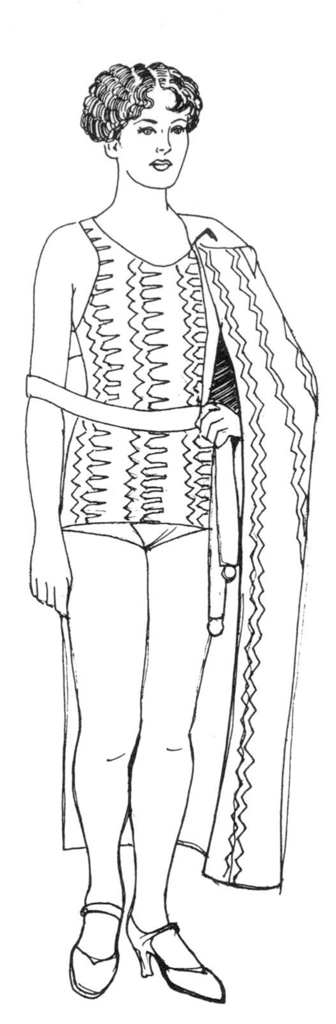

Tunic and knickers style bathing costume with matching bathing wrap, c. 1928

INFORMAL AND SPORTS WEAR

Blazers were worn with sports clothes and always had patch pockets.

By about 1920 jackets and breeches without skirts were occasionally seen for riding although it was more common to see an apron-skirted habit, so that just the front of the legs were covered. For riding astride, divided skirts or breeches were popular, although by the mid-1920s breeches worn with boots or jodhpurs were more fashionable.

For bathing or swimming, one piece costumes with skirts as well as tunic and knickers were worn in the early 1920s at which time they reached the knees. Gradually they became shorter until they just covered the upper part of the thighs. The costumes could be patterned with spots or stripes or even abstract designs. If belts were worn they were placed at whatever waistline was fashionable.

In the 1930s bathing suits were often made with divided skirt effects. The tops became less of a bodice style and could have shoulder straps. A brassière type top could even be worn with the pants resembling shorts. One-piece bathing costumes were cut low to allow for sunbathing which had recently become popular and were very often backless. Machine knitted wool was the most popular material used. Bathing caps which fitted close to the head were made of rubber and could be any colour.

Beach pyjamas became popular in the early 1930s and flannel slacks and divided skirts were also worn. Cotton dresses that buttoned down the front were often worn over these and left open from the waist. Linen or cotton dresses worn for beachwear were often backless with matching short jackets. Playsuits became modish around 1937. These consisted of shorts and shirts, either separate or joined, and could be worn with a wrap-over skirt to match.

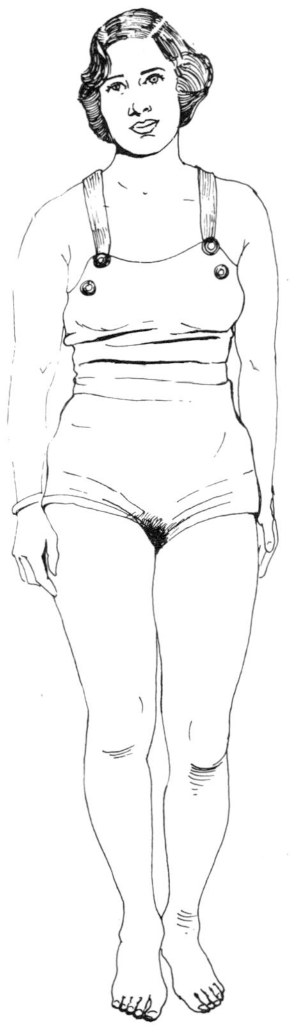

For golfing, tweed skirts with matching capes or coats were worn with shirts and ties. Cardigans and jerseys, sometimes knitted in Fair Isle patterns, were popular. Woollen stockings with checked designs were generally worn with stout rubber-soled shoes. From the mid 1920s Homburg hats or caps were replaced by cloche hats. In the 1930s suede tops were often worn with tweed skirts and the shirts were very often in a checked material. Instead of cloche hats, crocheted caps later became fashionable wear.

Tennis dresses usually had white collars and cuffs; blouses and skirts could also be worn. Tennis dresses in the early 1920s were about 25cm from the ground and by about 1925 had risen to just below the knees. They were usually in white, worn with white cardigans and white stockings and shoes. The skirts were mainly pleated to allow for freer movement. White trousers with turn-ups were also worn in the later 1920s. In the early 1930s tennis dresses were often sleeveless with a tucked bodice. The shorter skirts were pleated at the front, with two side pockets, and were usually worn with a belt.

Divided skirts and shorts became more popular around 1936 and were worn with ankle-length socks. The white tennis shoes were usually laced, but could occasionally be of the strapped variety.

By 1939, short circular or sunray pleated skirts with tight underpants were the mode and were worn with short-sleeved shirts.

Hair ribbons and bandeaux or small caps were worn to keep the hair in place in the early 1920s, but later on eyeshades on a band became fashionable.

For cycling, divided skirts or shorts were popular and

One-piece bathing costume with adjustable straps, c. 1935

On the left is a casual wear pair of decorative pyjamas, often worn for party wear, c. 1929. The lady in the centre is in a golfing outfit; suede or leather belted jacket, slim-fitting tweed skirt and a slouch hat worn at an angle, c. 1937. On the right the skating costume consists of a thick hip-length jumper with matching sleeveless woollen cardigan and scarf. The skirt is short and pleated. Tights and high boots with skates attached complete the ensemble, c. 1927

Boned corset, c. 1924

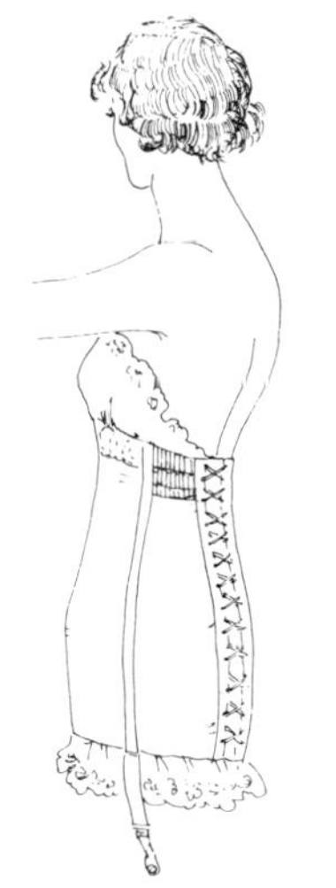
Back-laced evening undergarment with elasticated sides, c. 1920

Corset with adjustable suspenders, c. 1924

berets were also worn to keep the hair in place.

For motoring, clothes were simply the normal day wear, although a three-piece suit, comprising skirt, jumper and long coat was also worn. Leather coats could be worn on motoring journeys. Dust coats declined in popularity around 1939.

For skating, short pleated or flared skirts were worn with woollen jumpers and matching cloche hats and skating boots in the 1920s and 30s. A winter sport outfit comprised a long woollen pullover and trousers tucked into thick woollen socks. Woolly gloves, a large scarf and a peaked cap were also worn. Over the woollen pullover a jacket with pockets and fastened with a belt and large buttons could also be worn.

UNDERWEAR

In 1928 when dresses were straight and flowing, and reached just above the knees, underwear began to resemble the Greek undertunic. Cami-knickers, which were a type of loose knicker with flaps that fastened between the legs at almost mid-thigh and a petticoat top, were worn, and they were allowed to hang down loosely. Even suspender belts lost in favour, and it became fashionable to roll the stockings around garters above the knees. The only undergarment that remained close fitting was the brassière.

In the early 1930s cami-knickers were superseded by camisoles and knickers, which was, in fact, the cami-knickers in two separate parts. The legs of the knickers were lace frilled. Gradually panties, similar to children's ribbed cotton ones, became popular. They were shorter and better fitting, and often in a silky material.

OUTDOOR WEAR

The overcoats around 1919 were barrel shaped and gave emphasis to the hips by means of large pockets. They were usually of the wrap-over kind. Three-quarter length coats became popular around 1920. They were often waisted with large stand-up collars, or they could have capes attached. Looser *Raglan* type coats were popular. Both fur trimming and fur coats, usually three-quarter length, were also very fashionable.

Large collars were very fashionable in the 1920s on the popular loose coats. These were generally wrapped over and fastened with a large button at the waist or a little lower and could have a half belt at the back. Collars and cuffs and trimmings on pockets and hems were often of fur or fur imitations.

Coats were often made to match the dresses over which they were worn, or else the lining matched the lighter weight dress. Suede or leather coats became popular for sports wear.

Coats followed the length of dresses and the sleeves could be straight or bell shaped. Double-breasted Raglan or Chesterfield styles were still worn in the late 1920s, and scarf collars were also fashionable then.

In the early 1930s overcoats were mainly long and straight with high waistlines, collars that were high at the back and also revers. Raglan and Magyar sleeves were fashionable. Fur trimmings went out of fashion. The coats looked quite masculine in appearance. Some had no collars at all or had detachable scarf collars. Cape collars became popular around 1934, and scarves and bows were often worn at the neck.

Coats just shorter than the dresses worn beneath or three-quarter length swagger coats were worn from about 1934. From then on coats were made in all lengths and both fitted and loose coats were fashionable. Squarish shoulders became popular around 1936 and wide revers on coats became fashionable as did Indian lamb fur collars. By 1937 coats in general had become slightly shorter and box coats, which fell loose, were much worn. They could be single or double breasted.

Sleeves could be wide at the top, like leg-of-mutton or gigot type sleeves, or they could be long and tight with fur cuffs matching the fur collars. Dolman and bishop sleeves were also popular.

From about 1937 spring coats were made with an edge to edge closure with buttons and loops or a tie around the waist. In 1939, a military look was revived with epaulettes over straight and built-up shoulders and wide revers.

In inclement weather *mackintoshes* or waterproofs were made to fold up small enough to fit into a bag, and were made in a variety of colours. Raincoats were made of artificial silks, gabardine or other waterproof materials. They were made in a great variety of single- or double-breasted styles with or without belts, but a popular fashion was the trench coat.

FOOTWEAR

After the First World War crocodile as well as snakeskin and other exotic skins became the vogue for shoes. Handbags

Boned corset with side fastening, c. 1923

Elasticated girdle with a side laced fastening, c. 1925

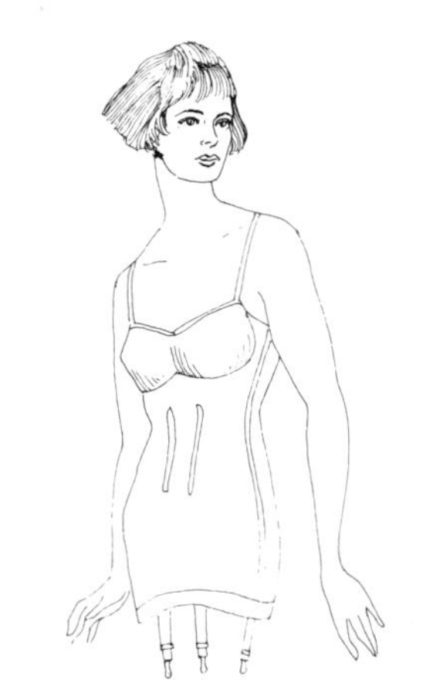

Elasticated undergarment with boned front, c. 1928

On the left the lady is in a single-breasted wrap-over coat with a deep collar and lapels. The coat is fastened at the low waist with a single large button. The hat is of the cloche style. The lady in the centre is also in a single-breasted wrap-over coat, with a stand-up collar and a large buckle fastening at the waist. The hat is a large picture style. The chauffeur is in livery of a long jacket and peaked cap, c. 1924

c. 1919

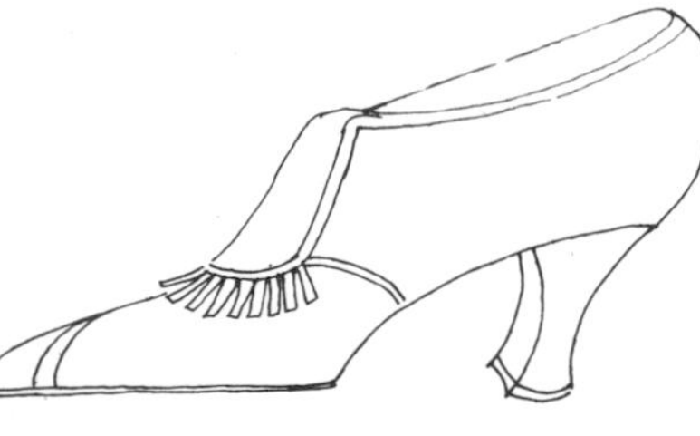

c. 1920

c. 1920-24

were also made of these skins to match the shoes, and were very fashionable amongst smart women. With the emancipation of women and their new-found freedom there were many experiments with different shoe styles, although basically all shoes had pointed toes, high-cut vamps and curved heels. Shoe fashions were not confined to the upper classes, but were also set by the younger generation of 'flappers'.

As methods of shoe manufacture progressed, so fashionable shoes became cheaper and within the reach of most people. Instead of shoes having to be made entirely by hand, they could now be machine made, thus cutting down costs and making it possible for many more styles to be produced. Although these shoes were not so hard wearing, it became feasible to change the styles more often.

Motoring, which was becoming part of everyday life, brought about new fashions, such as foot muffs, carriage boots and overshoes that were lined in a warm material. Women's footwear was made in a variety of materials: reversed leathers to form suede which could be used in conjunction with kid, patent leather and satins. Buckskin and antelope were also in vogue. Lizard, snakeskin, sharkskin, gabardine, as well as various cloths, were in great demand, and very often accessories such as handbags and gloves were made of matching materials. Apart from those matching the

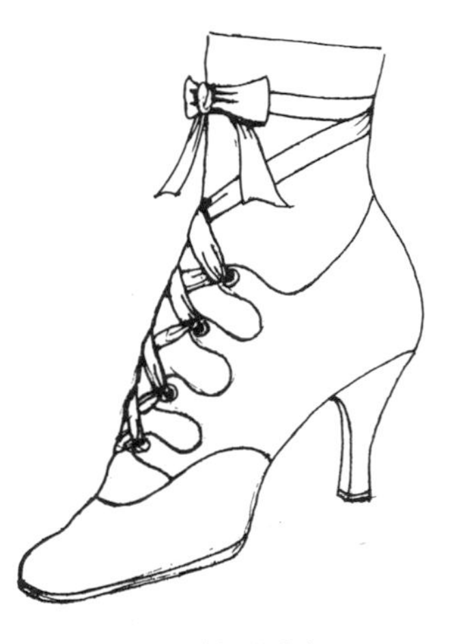

c. 1920-24

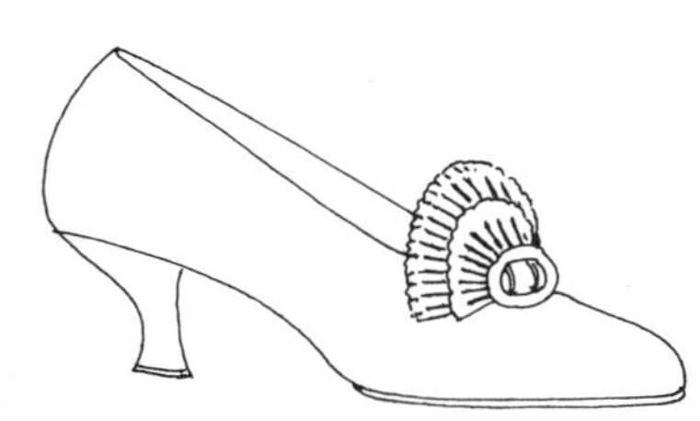

Black glacē kid court shoe, c. 1920-24

Ladies' patent leather shoe, c. 1920-24

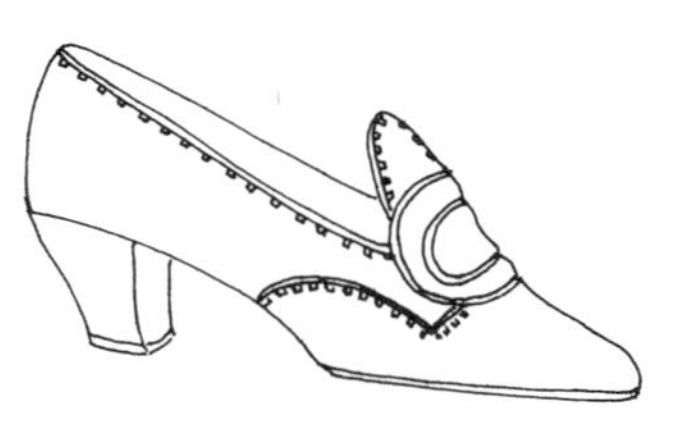

Black glacē kid court shoe, c. 1920-24

3 *The ladies are wearing dresses typical of the late 1920s. The skirts have reached knee length. The lady on the left is in a skirt with a godet front and inverted pleats. The jacket was loose fitting with a low V neckline showing the blouse beneath. On the right, the skirt has knife pleats in the front. The hip-length jumper blouse with a high V necked opening has small cuffed sleeves. Both wear close-fitting cloche type hats. c.1928.*

4 *On the right the lady is dressed in a leisure trouser suit with wide flared trousers of a patterned satin, a square shouldered jacket and a waist sash of matching colour. A high necked blouse is worn underneath. c.1937.*

The lady on the left is in the style of French fashion houses. The waistline is in the normal place and the V shaped opening has large lapels up to the shirt-topped buttoned bodice. The shoulders are squared, three-quarter length and puffed at the shoulders. She is wearing a large picture hat. c.1939.

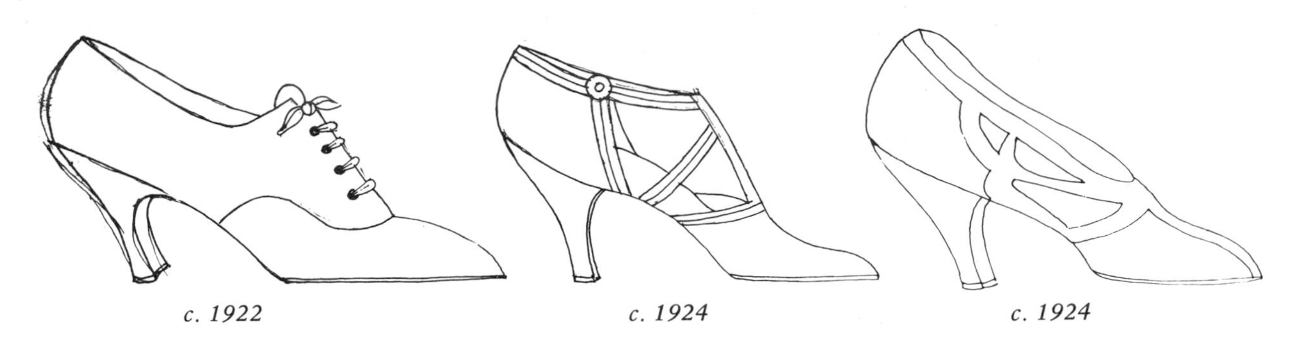

c. 1922 *c. 1924* *c. 1924*

c. 1922

c. 1924

colour of clothes, shoes in the earth colours such as sand, beige, brown, bronze and grey, were popular.

In the 1920s Gabrielle Chanel, apart from designing fashionable clothes, set the trend for open black and beige sling-back court shoes.

In the 1930s, platform soles made their appearance. These made women appear much taller. Carmen Miranda, a Mexican actress, made these extremely fashionable by adding diamanté or paste jewellery as well as different leathers and designs to the platforms, which at their most extreme could be 15cm from the ground. High wedges were also used to increase the height of heels, without having to raise the soles too far from the ground. The wedges could be ornamented in a variety of ways – by having designs sculpted on them or with different coloured layers of cloth or leather.

Thick high heels as well as a variety of T straps and ankle straps were also very popular on ladies' shoes.

With the popularity of the Russian Ballet, *Russian boots* reaching to mid-calf and made of leather became very fashionable. They were round-toed and flat-heeled, and although well fitting were wrinkled around the ankles.

Silk and lisle *stockings* played an important part in making legs look more attractive, as these were now more seen. Light coloured stockings in beige, grey or pink were very fashion-

c. 1925

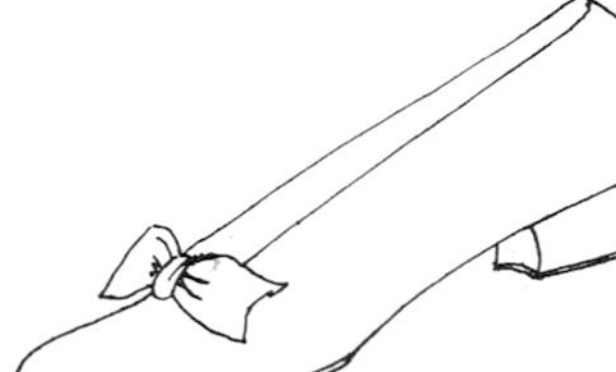

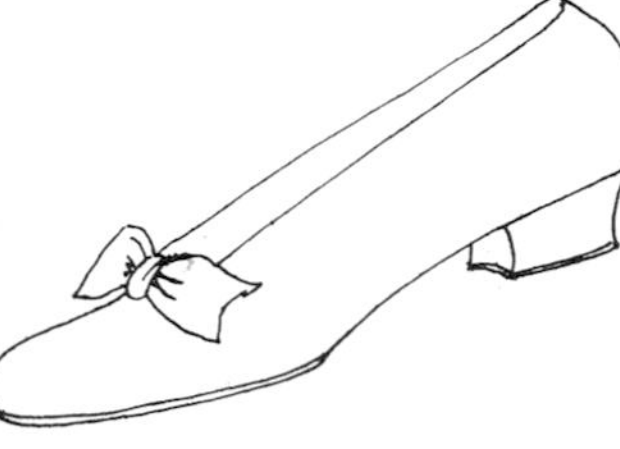

Slipper c. 1925-26

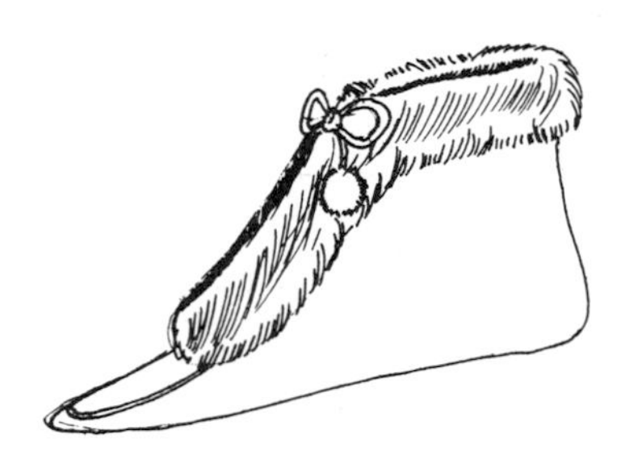

1925-26

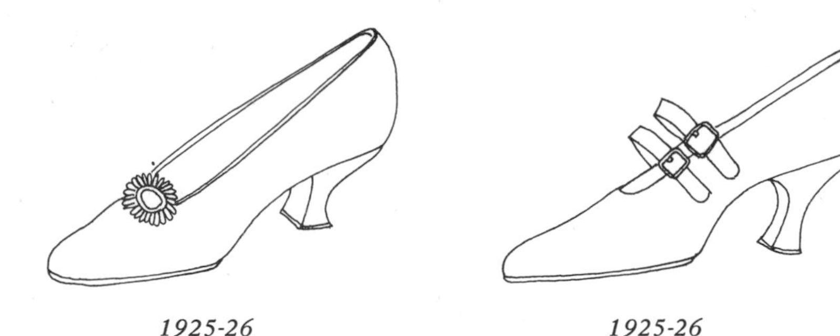

1925-26 1925-26

c. 1929

able in the 1920s, and by about 1923 coloured shoes also became popular.

The low heeled shoes popularised during the First World War were still fashionable, but with the toes more pointed. High-heeled court shoes or shoes with straps and cuban heels, about 4cm high, were also worn. Shoe uppers decorated with cut-out designs became very fashionable and the strapped shoes of this sort, where patterns were cut out of the toe-pieces and the sides, gradually developed into sandals in the 1930s.

With the popularity of the dances which would have been difficult to dance in high-heeled shoes – the Black Bottom and the Charleston – evening shoes were made in a sandal style with low heels, often of gold or silver kid. Heel heights were also affected by skirt lengths: as skirts lengthened again, heels became lower.

By the beginning of the 1930s the variety of shoe styles was great; there were high or low heels, pumps, sandals, slippers, shoes with ankle straps or instep straps and sling backs. They could be fastened with laces or buckles and made in many differing colours and materials. With the new greater ability of treating leathers, all kinds, including

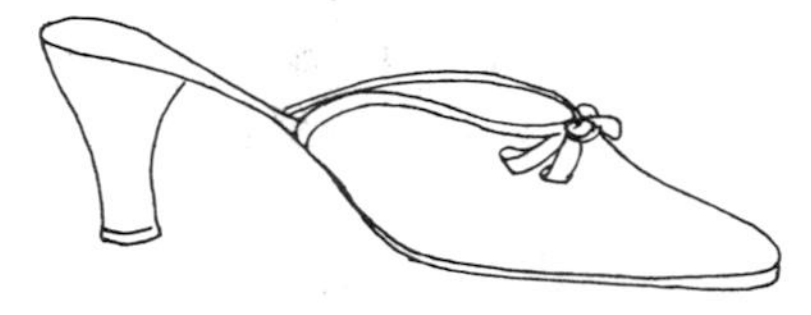

c. 1926

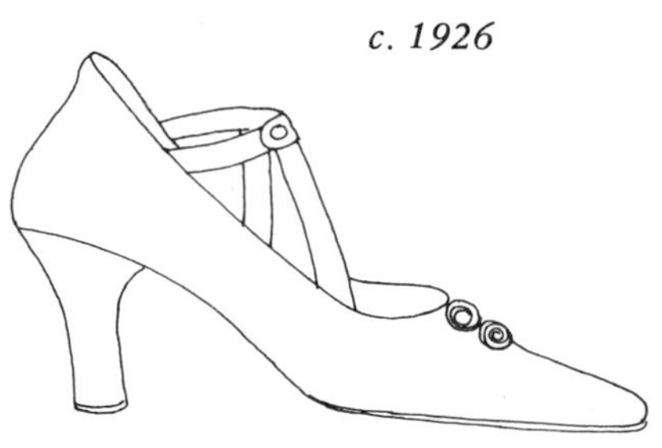

c. 1931

Two-tone shoes, c. 1931

Open shoe of brocade and gold kid, c. 1934

Thick platform sandals, c. 1939

Wooden-soled sandal, c. 1939

c. 1932

Suede shoes with straps and ribbon ties, c. 1931

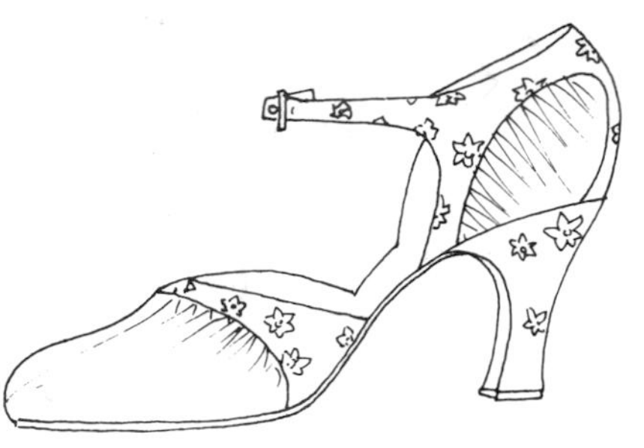

Open shoes made of kid and brocade, c. 1934

Silk braided hat with sealskin ornamentation, c. 1922

reptile skins, could be made pliable enough to use for shoes. Suede was often used and was trimmed with calfskin.

HEADWEAR

After the First World War wide-brimmed hats remained popular and were worn until the early 1920s. The brims could be pulled down over the brow. These soft hats were often made of cloth, wool or velour and were sometimes in mushroom or scuttle shapes. They could also be made close fitting. Berets worn pulled well down over to one side, tasselled caps and tam-o'-shanters were also worn. From about 1921 trimmings often projected beyond the brims and comprised feathers, flowers and bunches of fruit. Some hats were decorated with elaborate embroidery as well as appliqué work. For summer wear the brims were broader than in the winter when they were also turned up. Hats with wide brims were sometimes tilted forward so that their brims did not interfere with the high coat collars.

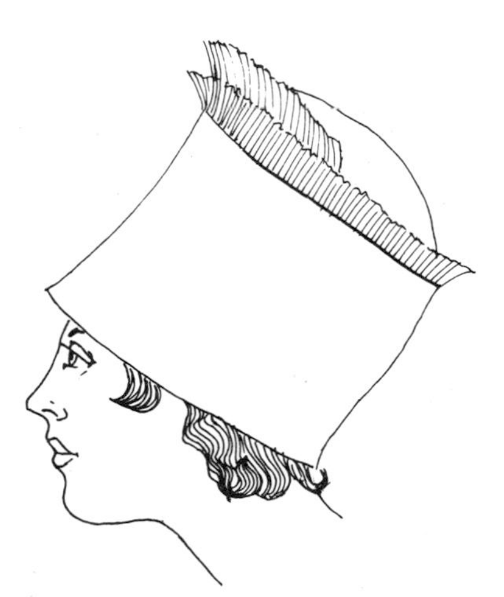

Round flower-pot style hat with top edged in organza pleating, c. 1921

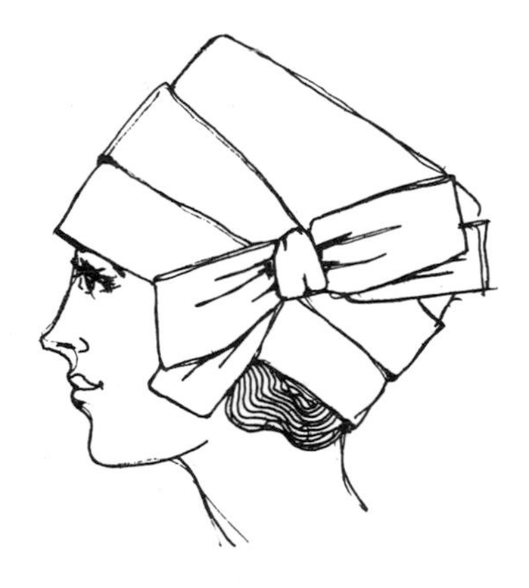

Flower-pot style hat with velvet hatband and bow, c. 1923

Round hat with turned-up brim, c. 1922

Turban-style hat with rolled-up brim and self trimmings, c. 1924

Inverted top-hat style with ribbon and bar ornamentation, c. 1924

Pull-on type hat with a stitched brim and floral decoration, c. 1924

For motoring and travelling in general, toques were popular. They were often made of a fine leather and had designs painted on them.

As short hair became fashionable cloche hats became the mode around 1923. They had deep crowns with narrow brims which could be turned down or up. These hats were pulled down over the head so far that the hair, except for the curls or waves on the cheeks, as well as most of the face, was concealed. Trimmings were generally quite flat, consisting of ribbons or materials such as felt or leather sewn on in various designs.

By about 1926 cloches were the prevailing style of headwear with the crown even deeper than previously. Brims were not always present, and if they were, they were usually quite small and down at the back with the front or side turned up. One variety of cloche was known as a 'helmet'.

Picture-hat style with trimmed hatband and bow, c. 1924

Turned-up brim style hat edged with ribbon and bow decoration, c. 1924

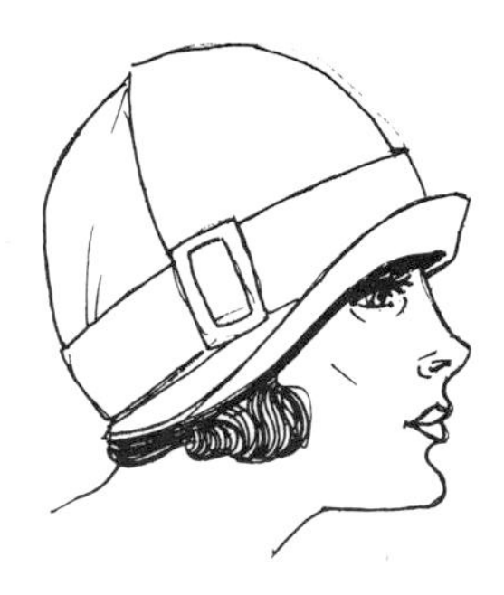

Cloche hat with a quartered crown and ribbon hatband and buckle, c. 1924

Hat with adaptable brim and ribbon hatband and loop decoration, c. 1924

Soft casual hat trimmed with a front bow and buckle, c. 1924

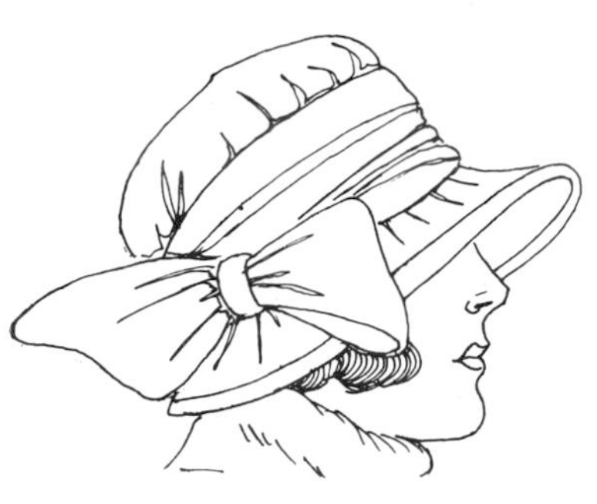

Dolly Varden style hat with trimmed and folded hatband ending in a large bow, c. 1925

Poke-bonnet style hat with folded hatband and bow, c. 1925

Hat made of silk plush trimmed with a self bow, c. 1925

The crowns of cloches were usually domed. For summer wear large picture hats were the general mode with ribbon or flower decorations, mainly on the left side.

By about 1928 hats could have the sides drooping with the brim longer to one side or the back rather like a sou'wester. Gradually the crowns became shallower and the brims larger. The really large brims were folded back on to the crown and draped at the sides, so that the face was again visible. Brims were sometimes uneven with the uneven cut parts turned up – holes could even be cut into the brims. Felt hats with the brims turned up in front and osprey feathers at the side were fashionable around 1927-1928. The helmet hats were worn with turned-up brims and domed hats usually had the brims down.

By the 1930s hats had a softer appearance and trimmings

Large picture hat with centre open brim decorated with a large feather in the hatband, c. 1927

Deep-crowned cloche hat with a turned-up brim, c. 1924

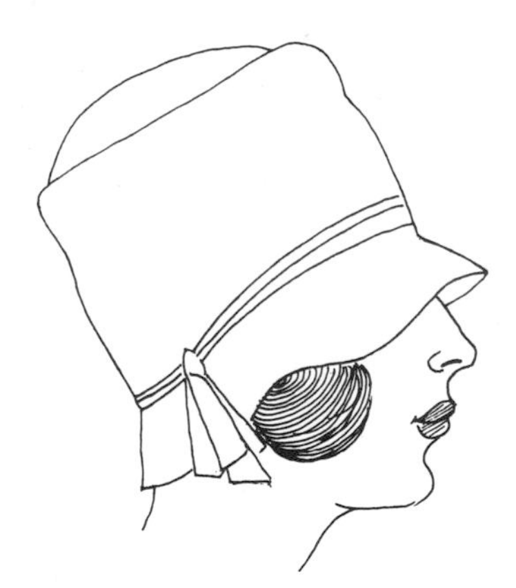

Deep-crowned cloche hat with a turned-down brim, c. 1924

Deep cloche hat with scalloped turned-up brim with side feather decoration, c. 1925

Deep cloche hat with hatband of silk and flowing ends, c. 1928

again consisted of flowers and feathers worn on the large brims. The shallower crowns fitted the head closer, the brim turned up in front but coming down at the sides over the ears. This gave the hats the appearance of tilting back slightly.

Berets, sometimes knitted, which were first worn in the 1920s, became quite fashionable from the 1930s. *Turban* hats were also popular. These had the crown covered in a soft material with long loose ends that could either be tied in a bow or swathed around the head like a turban. In the early 1930s hats became quite small with small brims or even without any at all. These types of hats were worn on one side or at an angle. Short veils, just reaching the eyes, often went with them.

Pill box style hats also became popular, and knitted hats were also still being worn, as well as the Breton sailor styles which had been popular in straw and other materials since the beginning of the century.

Crocheted hats, caps and berets were also in the mode. Suede cloches and hats were worn for sporting occasions. 1934 saw the introduction of the Tyrolean hats. For winter wear astrakhan or fur hats were worn, and were sometimes called cossacks. Fez shapes as well as the tricorne forms were still popular.

Although hats were still worn tilted, about 1935 low crowned hats with fairly high brims as well as halo berets made their appearance. By 1936 crowns were higher and could be pointed in a Robin Hood style. The crowns could be pleated or made with tucks. These hats were usually made of a felt or suede. Berets began to decline in popularity.

Woollen cloche pull-on type hat with silk hatband, c. 1929

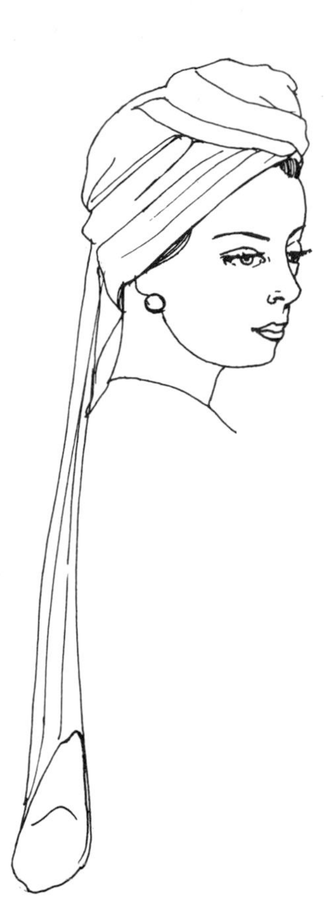

Turban-style headdress with long flowing streamer, c. 1938

Slouch felt hat with feathers, worn at an angle, c. 1935

Hats were worn mainly off the face about 1937, and were made in varying shapes and styles. Halo hats or Breton sailor hats with the brims turned up were also in fashion. Slouched felt hats were worn in the last two years of the 1930s and hats could also be worn at an angle. Snoods and hoods as well as jersey turbans with scarves attached were amongst the many types of headwear worn in the winter of 1939, and hats were again perched forward. Small caps or berets usually had a band at the back to hold them on. Brown or black elastic, to match the hair colouring, could also be used and was attached either side of the hat and worn drawn under the hair at the back.

Veils, either long or short, were fashionable trimmings; they could be eye level or reach to the nose. If longer, the veil reached under the chin and was tied behind.

Most hats of this period were worn well down; even straw hats had downward curving brims which could be flower or ribbon trimmed. Just after this fashion, the leghorn, made of a bleached wheat, was popular. A cheaper version of leghorn straw was Tuscan straw. This style of hat was more becoming and was made of an openwork design with the brim curled slightly upwards.

For evening wear bandeaux or forehead bands which could be embellished with feathers or plumes were popular until the 1930s. Sequined turbans or turbans adorned with aigrettes became fashionable in the early 1920s. Later on in the era it became unnecessary to wear any headwear in the evenings, although flowers, ribbons and sequined veils were worn.

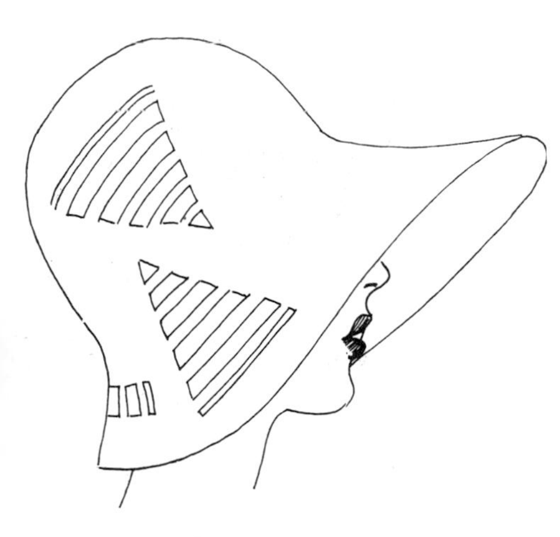

Domed hat with large turned-down brim, c. 1929

Close-fitting turban-type hat, c. 1929

High slouched hat worn at an angle, c. 1939

Felt top-hat style with leaning crown and a feather ornament in the hatband, worn at an angle on the side of the head, c. 1935

From the mid-1930s turbans were worn at cocktail parties. Around 1935 Juliet caps made their appearance. These were small round skull caps adorned with sequins, beads or pearls and worn with the hair forming a kind of halo of curls around it.

By about 1880 the custom of wearing indoor caps had fallen into decline apart from being worn by domestic servants and nurses (who still wear caps today). Waitresses also wore a type of cap until the beginning of the Second World War. Boudoir caps might be worn in the 1920s as either night caps or dressing caps to protect the hair whilst sleeping or when placing garments over the head.

After 1918, for weddings, small lace caps or long white veils were worn as well as the traditional wreaths of flowers.

Hand-knitted beret with a decorative edge design and a pom-pon on the top, c. 1930

HAIRSTYLES

From about 1918 to 1925 women often went to gentlemen's barber shops to have their hair cut in the fashionable 'boyish' bob which was known as French bob, straight bob, shingle, etc.

Around 1919 hair was worn set in tight waves with the bulk of the hair in deep waves over the forehead and the sides waved or curled. Fringes were also popular. The back hair could be dressed fairly high and held in place with combs. When short styles became fashionable, the parting was generally to one side, usually the left, and held with a comb or slide. False hair coils with curls could be pinned to the back. Short bobbed hairstyles became popular in the early 1920s with the hair close to the nape of the neck and the tips of the ears visible. The back was often worn in a loose chignon, this effect being achieved with a hairpiece.

Small silk toque hat worn perched on the side of the head, c. 1939

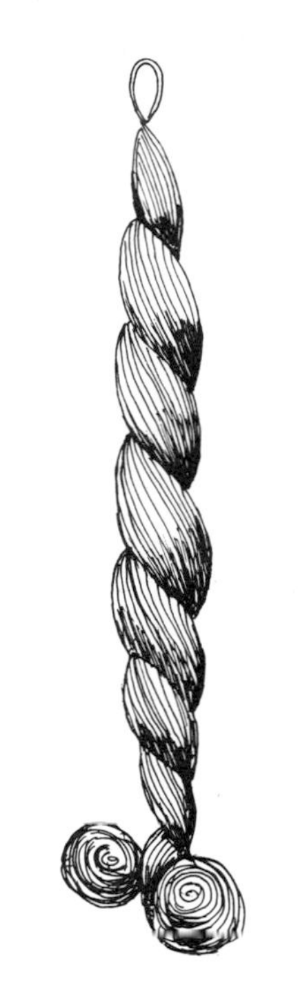

Hairpiece, c. 1925

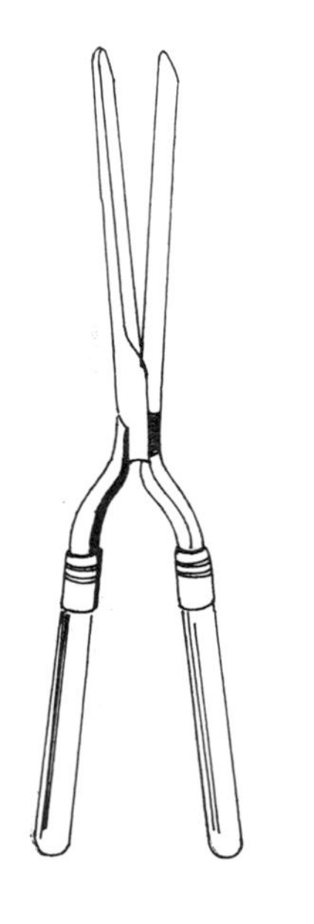

Curling tongs, c. 1925

One method of cutting the hair was by having it cut quite short all round, with the ends 'clubbed'; later, when hair-cutting became more skilled, many varying styles were devised.

Coiled plaits were worn around the ears and known as earphones. This was also a popular style for ladies who preferred to keep their hair long. Another way to give the impression of short hair was to wear it in a tight curl rolled under or plaited and braided and worn close to the head.

For evening wear ornamentation varied from gold scarves wound round the head and decorated with upstanding feathers to jewelled diadems with cascades of plumes trailing down to the shoulders.

When the puffed-out hairstyles were gradually replaced by the sleeker styles, they were sometimes known as Chinese or Japanese styles, as the hair was drawn back from the front and dressed in a bun at the back which could be adorned with flowers, fans or feathers. This style remained popular for quite a while.

About 1921 a looser hair fashion became the mode; this was a fluffier bob, giving a wind-blown appearance.

For evening wear long chiffon scarves could be tied around the coiffure and allowed to flow freely.

Postiches and torsades were still popular worn across the forehead; a postiche being a hair piece, whilst a torsade was also false hair, consisting of two pieces of hair twisted together and curled at either side.

In 1923 it was fashionable to wear a wide band around the head and across the forehead. This became so popular that bandeaux were designed with embroidery and also encrusted with paste jewel designs.

In 1924 the shingle hairstyle was the rage, with a fringe also being popular. The cut of the hair was such that it was tapered, exposing all the ends to view. The hair was worn either straight or waved encircling the head. Quite often the women's hair was shorter at the back than men's. The side hair, which was longer and in waves, was sometimes attached to the cheeks with the aid of a plaster. There were many variations of the shingle, with the hair cut to form a point at the centre back, gradually merging into the Eton crop fashion from about 1925. This style was rather boyish in appearance, cut straight and above ear level with the sides later left longer, so that they could be made to curl forward onto the cheeks.

For evening wear a postiche was often added to give these very short hairstyles a longer appearance, and by about 1927 the shingle was softened with soft curls on top, thus making the style more feminine.

Around 1929 hair became slightly longer with soft curls towards the forehead and by about 1930 styles were really quite a bit longer with forehead waves and small clusters of curls at the back and sides, therefore a postiche was no longer necessary and gradually became unfashionable. Permanent waves had by now been perfected; they were cheaper and quicker than previously, and so their use became quite widespread. Blonde hair popularised by film stars like Jean Harlow also became the mode, so hair was frequently dyed this colour.

From about 1930 to 1935 hair became more sculptured in appearance with waves or rolls at the back and curls or flat pin curls at the back and sides. A trend for upswept hair also emerged. During the early 1930s bobbed hairstyles as well as variations of the shingle were worn. As methods of hair tapering evolved, hair was left longer at the nape of the neck so that it could be formed into curls. Pin curls also became fashionable as well as deep waves. All these styles were now easier to carry out with the aid of perms and Marcel waving as well as water waves and hair setting.

Long bobbed hairstyles were popularised by the famous film actress Greta Garbo around 1932; for these the hair was combed behind the ears and loose curls were worn at the nape.

For evening wear tiaras as well as floral wreaths and ornamental bandeaux were worn.

Towards 1937 a popular fashion was a curled or rolled fringe on the forehead with the back hair worn in a pageboy bob. With the longer hair quite often only the ends were permed which allowed for a sleek effect on the head. Another modish style was the hair worn piled on the top of the head and held there with ornamental combs and pins. This upswept style could have been created to accommodate the tiaras and coronets worn in the coronation year of 1937. Another popular style was with a centre parting with the hair smooth on top and curls framing the face.

By 1939, just before the Second World War, simpler hairstyles prevailed. The styles had a more sophisticated look with waves across the head and longer hair at the

Short hairstyle with wind-blown appearance, c. 1920

Decorative Spanish-style comb worn in the hair, c. 1920

Tiara-type band covering a short hairstyle, c. 1923

Bobbed hairstyle, c. 1922

Fringed short hair style, c. 1924

Narrow band worn around the head and across the forehead, c. 1924

back in ringlets and tied with a bow. Net snoods were also beginning to be worn to contain the hair. The hair was swept away from the face with curls at the sides, the longer hair being gathered into a snood. Veronica Lake, a famous American film star, started a fashion for long, loose shoulder-length hair that was turned under at the ends and hung over one side of the face. This style was soon discouraged as the loose, flopping hair was found to be dangerous when women worked on machinery during the war. Therefore snoods or scarves worn around the head were introduced.

BEAUTY AIDS

After the First World War a new cosmetic fashion came into being, that of rouging the lips. Vivid lip colouring was first fashionable in the 1920s, when lipstick became the most popular form of make-up. Eye make-up was also important. An eyebrow pencil was used to form a thin arched line over the eyebrows, where they had been plucked. Eyebrow pencils were also used to draw patches over moles on the face to resemble beauty spots. Lips were painted into the shape of a cupid's bow, and when this fashion went into decline, eyebrow shapes became more exaggerated.

The basic face colour was very pale, emphasised with pink powder and rouge on the cheeks. Sunburnt complexions were not fashionable until the 1930s. Eyelids were coloured for evening, whilst in the daytime they were given a shiny appearance with lanolin. Mascara was used to darken the eyelashes, whilst eyedrops were used to give a sparkle to the eyes themselves.

In the Edwardian era women had tried to make themselves look more mature, but in the 1920s the accent was on youth. This encouraged the use of a whole new range of cosmetic preparations designed to keep the youthful complexion and discourage wrinkles. Face-lifts became fashionable for the older ladies, and although plastic surgery was still in its infancy, much had been learned from operations on the wounded soldiers of the First World War. Dental techniques had also improved and it was possible to correct and disguise bad teeth with artificial coverings.

Advances in chemistry also played an important part in the development of cosmetics, enabling them to be made of more subtle materials, and powders could now be made of finer materials and blended into a greater variety of shades. Lipsticks could also be made in a wider range of reds, and they were manufactured to harmonise with the rest of the make-up used, and also the colour of clothes worn.

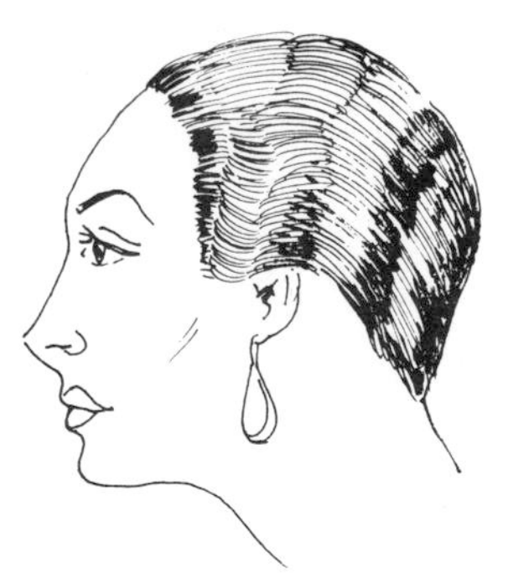

Eton crop with soft waves, c. 1925

ACCESSORIES

Gloves again became popular for evening wear just after the First World War, as did mitts in black or white lace. Evening gloves in the 1920s and 30s were still long and could have as many as 20 buttons. They were often decorated with beads and embroidery.

For winter wear gloves were often of a knitted wool and lined for extra warmth. Leather and fur were also popular and in the 1920s string gloves were worn for riding.

Gloves in the 1920s were generally fairly plain. Buttoning on gloves for everyday wear became rarer as they began to have elastic insets at the wrists. Gauntlet gloves were also worn quite frequently. In the late 1920s gloves and stockings were often of the same colour.

Fringed straight and short hairstyle, c. 1925

Leather handbags were usually mounted on metal frames with snap closures and handles to match. Silk handbags were popular with light dresses and often matched them. Around 1926 flat handbags, without a handle, were envelope shaped; these were also usually mounted on metal frames. Many bags were in a softer leather or cloth and might have tortoise-shell frames. From around 1926 some leather bags, instead of a frame closure, had zip fasteners. By 1929 it was the mode for handbags and shoes to match in colour and material.

Evening handbags were often in brocade, but could also be embroidered in *petit point*. Metal and beaded bags and chain metal bags were also fashionable. These usually had metal frames with a thin metal chain for carrying. Many bags were made in a gold or silver mesh. Some bags were fairly small and known as vanity bags. In the mid-1930s most bags were fairly small and envelope shaped. These were known as *pochettes*. After about 1936 hangbags became larger and were made in various shapes.

Soft waves piled on top of head and short back and sides, c. 1925

Muffs and *stoles* were fashionable periodically and were made of feathers or fur. Around 1921 stoles and neckwear were often of fox fur. They were sometimes made like a shoulder cape with the fox head at the centre back and the front fastened with paws over hooks and eyes. The fur cape itself was usually composed of bushy tails. Embroidered and decorated Spanish-style shawls were fashionable for evening wear, often with long fringes.

Neck ruffles were popular for a brief while in the early

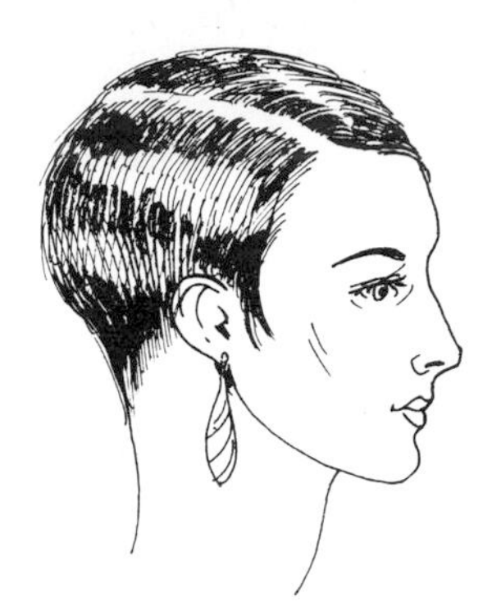

Eton crop hairstyle, c. 1926

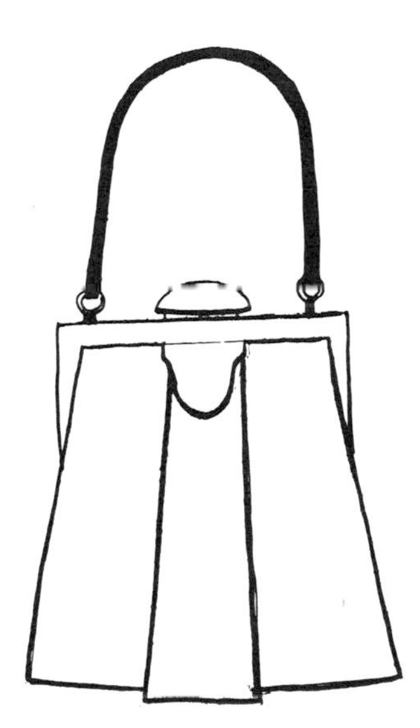

Soft leather handbag, c. 1920

Shingle style with soft waves, c. 1929

1920s. Silk scarves were worn in the daytime whilst for evening wear they were mainly of gauze or chiffon and could be draped loosely to one shoulder. In the 1920s scarves were often worn and knotted at the base of V-necked dresses or blouses. From around 1924 they sometimes had hand painted designs or could be in a batik. Jabots and fichus as well as georgette fill-ins were worn until the 1920s but gradually lost favour in the 1930s. Collars and cuffs, usually in white linen, were popular with tailored dresses and outfits.

Handkerchiefs were often visible above the outside breast pocket of tailored suit jackets around 1926.

Umbrellas were used for rainy weather and parasols against the sunshine. For the Ascot races, garden parties and other formal social occasions the sunshades or *parasols* were mainly of silk or chiffon. Raffia sunshades embroidered in different coloured raffias were fashionable for general everyday use. In the 1930s parasols were less used, but fashionable ladies were still seen with them occasionally, made of lace and organdie to match the fashionable summer dresses.

Umbrellas were long-handled with crook tops, or plain and straight. They could also have gold or ornamented handles. From around 1923 umbrellas became shorter and were usually in black or other sombre colours. Collapsible or telescopic handles with sliding and extending ribs were first seen in the mid-1920s. By the mid-1930s umbrellas were made in brighter colours to match the mackintoshes with which they were used.

Fans enjoyed a brief spell of popularity for evening wear in the early 1920s. They were of the folding variety and often made of ostrich feathers.

In the 1920s belts made either of leather of self material were worn at hip level. They were fastened with metal or tortoiseshell buckles or clasps. Belts could be either narrow or wide and even shaped.

Clasps, brooches, necklaces, bracelets, rings and earrings were all worn throughout the period. Diamonds and pearls were the most popular items of jewellery. Long pendant earrings became very fashionable in the 1920s. Brooches were worn on the shoulder and corsage and were generally rectangular in shape from the later 1920s. Slave-type bracelets showing an Oriental influence were much worn. Gold and jewelled anklets were also popular in the 1920s.

Beads and artificial pearls both for long and 'choker' necklaces were worn mainly with tailor-made suits. Crystal was sometimes used instead of more precious stones and could be set in rings or threaded as a necklace, sometimes with jet between. In the 1930s glass jewellery was imported from Czechoslovakia. Short double rows of pearls fastened at the back with a diamond clasp were popularised in the 1930s by Princess Marina, the wife of the Duke of York. Lapel pins or clips were often worn in place of brooches. Wood and cork jewellery was very popular for beach wear in the 1930s.

Zip fasteners were first manufactured around 1919 and were used on skirt and dress openings, but did not come into general use until the late 1920s. Hooks and eyes and bars were the usual fastenings for dresses and skirts. Press studs or *poppers* were also used. Fastening was generally on the left side or at the back. However, many of the straight tubular dresses had no openings and were made to put on over the head. Coat frocks and some casual dresses were open down the entire front and were usually closed with buttons, although zips were occasionally used. In the 1930s poppers became more popular than hooks and eyes, although on skirts where zip fasteners were used a hook and eye was generally used at the top of the placket.

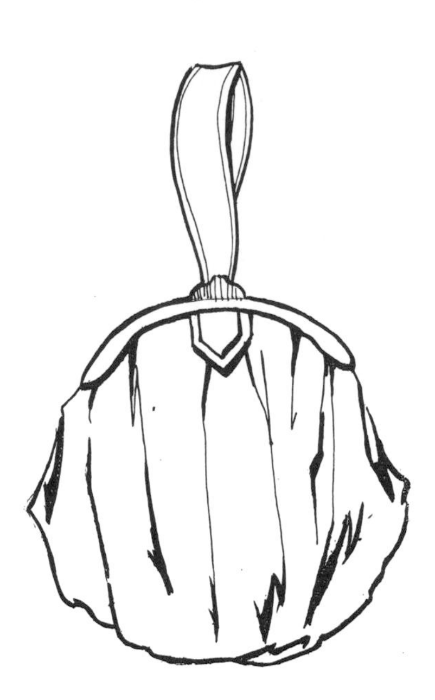

Stiff leather handbag with metal frame and clasp and leather handle, c. 1926

Decorated kid glove, c. 1929

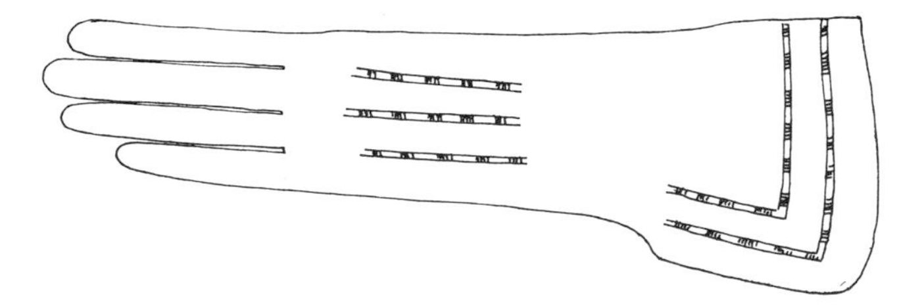

Gauntlet glove, c. 1929

Children

Young girl in above-the-knee-length dress with the waistline at hip level and wearing a large bow in her hair, c. 1922

Boys' and girls' clothes began to differ. Small boys stopped wearing skirts from about 1918 and their hair, which had been long, gradually became shorter until, by the end of the 1920s, it was cut as short as the men's.

By the 1930s boys' suits consisted of a long tunic or jersey worn with knee length trousers.

Girls wore short cotton dresses and sandals, without socks, in the summer. By the 1920s girls' dresses had become much shorter, and the three-quarter length socks previously so popular became ankle socks, thus more of the legs showed. Patterned and flowered materials again became fashionable,

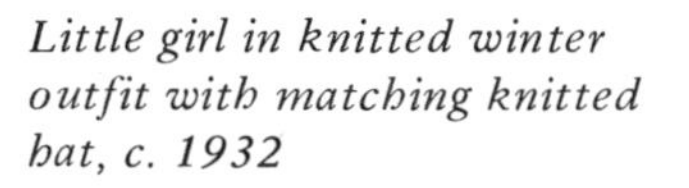

Little girl in knitted winter outfit with matching knitted hat, c. 1932

Small girl in beach costume and sun hat, c. 1932

Small boy in knitted suit and beret, c. 1932

Little girl in short smocked dress, c. 1932

Boy in short-trousered flannel suit, c. 1928

Boy wearing Norfolk jacket with breeches and high gaiters, c. 1922

Young girl in school uniform: velour round hat with school hatband, blazer with the usual patch pockets, and a knee-length gymslip, c. 1937

after a period of plain and pastel shades. Plaids and ginghams were also in vogue. Due to the popularity of hand knitting which had begun during the war, it was fashionable for children to wear knitted dresses and jumpers.

Also by the 1920s the longer hair of the early 1900s had become so short, and the hair ribbons worn so large and wide, that the wearing of hats became unpopular.

Little boy in overcoat with fly front fastening and patch pockets, worn with large cloth cap, c. 1920

Small boy in striped blazer with short trousers and cap, c. 1926

Girl in knee-length overcoat with half belt at the back, worn with long gaiters buttoned at the side and flower-pot style hat with turned-down brim, c. 1918

Glossary

Accordion pleats	Close pleats resembling the folds of an accordion
Appliqué	Flat decoration of material sewn to garment
Bandeau	Band or ribbon worn around the head to keep the hair in place
Basque	Extension with a fullness below the waistline of a jacket or bodice
Batik	Fabric dyed to give a marbled effect
Batswing sleeve	Sleeve fitted into an armhole reaching from shoulder to waist ending with a wrist band or cuff
Beret	Round piece of material gathered to a band to fit the head with a small point at the centre top
Bishop sleeve	Full sleeve gathered to a tight wristband or cuff
Blazer	Single- or double-breasted informal jacket with three patch pockets and buttons usually of metal
Boater	Stiff straw hat with flat crown and brim
Bob	Short hair cut to a V at the nape of the neck, softer than the Eton crop and shingle styles
Bolero	Short above-waist open jacket, usually sleeveless, with square or rounded fronts
Bow tie	Small tie made into a bow at the neck
Bowler hat	Felt hat with low round crown and narrow brim, also known as a Derby
Box coat	Short box-shaped coat
Box pleat	Two parallel pleats in opposite directions
Brassière	Undergarment shaped to support the bust
Breton sailor	Wide-brimmed sailor type hat
Brogues	Heavy shoes with designs punched in the leather tops
Bulldog shoe	Shoe with a deep boxed toe
Button stand	Separate strip of cloth sewn to the front of a coat to carry the buttons and buttonholes

Camisole	Undergarment worn over a corset for extra warmth
Cardigan	Close-fitting knitted jacket
Chemisette	Material fill-in for a dēcolletage
Chesterfield coat	Knee-length overcoat, usually with a fly front
Cloche hat	Bell-shaped close-fitting hat worn well down
Clocks	Decorative embroidery on socks
Coat frock	Front-buttoned frock in a heavy material, also worn outdoors without a coat
Co-respondent shoe	Two-toned shoe with toecap and counter in a different colour to the remainder of shoe
Counter	Overlaid piece at the back of the shoe upper
Covert coat	Shortish top coat
Cowl neckline	Loose folded and draped neckline
Cuff link	Ornamental buttons, usually gold or silver, joined by a short chain to a bar or other button, fastening together cuffs which have a buttonhole each side of the opening
Darts	Pointed tuck of material sewn together to give a better fit to a garment
Dēcolletage	Low-cut neckline
Diamantē	Imitation diamonds
Dinner jacket	Dress coat without tails, similar to a smoking jacket, with a silk rolled collar
Dirndl	Austrian Tyrol type skirt, full-gathered at the waist
Dolman sleeve	Cut in one with the body of the bodice to give a deep armhole
Dorothy Bag	Open topped handbag closed with a drawstring and held by the loop
Dress coat	Similar to a frock coat
Dust coat	Lightweight overcoat worn for protection against dust, especially when motoring
Epaulettes	Ornamental shoulder pieces
Fair Isle	Intricate knitted designs originating in the Scottish islands
Fly	An overlap of material to conceal buttons on coats, trousers and skirts
Four-in-hand	Necktie tied in a slip knot
Frock coat	Double-breasted jacket with long skirts, equally long front and back
Frogging	Ornamental braid and loops
Fringe	Hair cut short over the forehead in front, falling down either straight or curled
Gaiters	Material or leather covering for legs and shoe tops, buttoned on the outside and held in place under the foot with a strap
Gauging	Similar to smocking, with the fullness gathered in parallel rows of stitching

Gauntlet	Glove with a long cuff
Godet	Fluted pleat on lower part of skirt or sleeve to give extra fullness
Gore	Triangular piece of material inserted to give fullness without bulk
Helmet hat	Close-fitting hat worn with the sides extending over the ears
Hobble skirt	Very narrow skirt, tapering at the ankles
Homburg	Felt hat with a dent in the crown from front to back and a ribbon-edged brim curled up at the sides
Inverted pleat	Like a box pleat with the parallel pleats in reverse, the folds meeting on the face
Jabot	Lace or material cravat worn as a fill-in or decoratively on the bodice front
Jersey	Knitted woollen garment
Jetted	Piped or bound with a strip of self material
Jodhpurs	Riding breeches full to the knees & then right to the ankle held down with a strap under the foot; also ankle-high riding boots
Juliet cap	Close-fitting cap covered with bead or jewelled embroidery
Jumper	Loose blouse or pullover, usually of wool
Jumper dress	One-piece dress of knitted material
Knickerbockers	Loose knee breeches tightened at the knees with a band
Knife pleats	Folds of material folded over so that only one crease shows, all pointing in one direction
Lounge coat	Single- or double-breasted jacket without a waist seam, mainly worn on informal occasions
Magyar sleeve	Similar in cut to the Dolman, but closer fitting
Medici collar	High standing at the back, lower at the front
Mitts	Fingerless gloves
Monk shoe	Low plain shoe with buckle fastening
Morning coat	Coat with fronts cut away to the tails at the back which have a centre vent
Muffs	Rolls, often of fur, made open at either end to place the hands inside, suspended around the neck to waist level
Norfolk jacket	Jacket box-pleated front and back with pockets and a belt
Notch	V shape where the collar and edge of jacket or lapel meet
Oxford bags	Trousers with extremely wide flared bottoms
Oxford shoes	Shoes tied with laces, the fronts of the shoes stitched over facings which carry the holes for the laces
Panama hat	Straw hat made of plaited fibre from the toquilla leaf
Panties	Knickers with a side placket fastened with tiny buttons on one side of the waist (later elastic was used). The leg part was slightly flared
Peter Pan collar	Round collar with rounded ends in front, named after *Peter Pan* by Sir James Barrie

Pillbox	Small stiff round hat without a brim
Pinafore dress	Sleeveless dress worn over a blouse with a bib-like front
Piping	Edging made of narrow bias, usually folded over a thin cord
Platform sole	Sole and heel made in one, built up under instep and heel
Plus fours	Type of voluminous knickerbockers or breeches reaching to four inches below the knees
Pompadour	Hair brushed off the face and high coiffure
Pork pie hat	Low-crowned felt hat with a creased top
Postiche	Artificial hairpiece added to own hair
Princess line	Fitted style without a waist seam, the skirt and bodice cut in one
Pullover	Jumper without any fastening at all, slipped on over the head
Pumps	Low-cut shoe with low heels and thin soles
Pyjamas	Loose jacket and trousers
Raglan	Sleeve cut in one with the shoulder joining the top of the garment front and back
Reefer	Short, usually double-breasted overcoat or jacket
Revers	Turned-back front edges of a coat, jacket or bodice, often called lapels
Sailor collar	Collar, square at the back, narrowing to a point at the centre front
Shingle	Very short hairstyle shaped to the head, just covering the ears and coming to a point at the back
Shirring	Rows of gathering, similar to gauging
Shorts	Short trousers worn for casual and sports wear
Silk hat	Top hat
Slippers	Low-cut soft slip-on shoe for indoor wear
Smock	Yoked dress or shirt
Smocking	Stitching in a honeycomb pattern, alternately dividing and holding together tiny pleats.
Smoking jacket	Jacket similar to a lounge jacket
Snap brim	Soft felt hat with brim pulled down in front
Snood	Fine material or net to contain the hair
Sou'wester	Weatherproofed hat with slanting brim, longer at the back
Spats	Short ankle gaiters with buttons on the outside and a strap under the shoe
Step collar	Meeting lapel with a V notch
Stole	Long straight scarf, often with fringed ends, made of fur or material, worn over the shoulders
Suspender belt	Type of garter belt around the waist with longish elastic strips to hold up stockings. The elastic has metal and rubber clips to grip the stockings
Swagger coat	Loose coat, flaring from shoulder to hem
Sweater	Knitted or crocheted blouse or jacket style

Tail coat	Jacket with swallow tails at the back, the fronts cut short
Tailor-made	Suit made to measure, comprising jacket and skirt
Tam-O'-Shanter	Soft, knitted flat type of cap, usually of wool, with a pom-pon on top
Teagown	Informal full-length dress, usually yoked and allowed to hang loose with full sleeves
Toecap	Front upper part of shoe by the toe, sometimes of a contrasting colour
Toupee	Patch of false hair to cover a bald patch
Trench coat	Army type coat with shoulder flaps
Trilby	Soft felt hat
Turban	Oriental type headdress with material folded around the head
Turn-ups	Base of trousers turned up
Turtle neck	High turn-over collar
Tyrolean hat	Wide-brimmed felt or straw hat with a feather on one side
Ulster coat	Loose-fitting overcoat, usually with a belt or half belt, occasionally with a hood or cape
Vent	Vertical slit from the hem up
Wedge heel	Wooden or leather heel and sole in one piece, flat on the ground
Wing collar	High and stiff collar with the corners turned back
Yoke	Top part of garment to which the lower part is sewn

Select Bibliography

Amphlett, Hilda, *Hats*, Richard Sadler 1974

Arnold, J., *Handbook of Costume*, Macmillan 1973;
Patterns of Fashion, 2 Vols., Macmillan 1972

Asser, Joyce, *Historic Hairdressing*, Pitman 1966

Bennett-England, Rodney, *Dress Optional*, Peter Owen 1967

Boucher, F., *History of Costume in the West*, Thames & Hudson 1967;
20,000 Years of Fashion, Abrams

Bradfield, N., *Costume in Detail, Women's Dress 1730-1930*, Harrap 1968;
Historical Costumes of England, Harrap 1958

Braun-Ronsdorf, M., *The Wheel of Fashion*, Thames & Hudson 1964

Brooke, Iris, *Footwear*, Pitman 1972; *History of English Costume*, Methuen 1937;
English Children's Costume, A. & C. Black 1965

Buck, Anne, *Victorian Costume & Costume Accessories*, Herbert & Jenkins 1961
Calthrop, D.C., *English Dress from Victoria to George V*, Hall & Chapman 1934
Carter, Ernestine, *Twentieth-Century Fashion*, Eyre Methuen 1975
Contini, M., *The Fashion from Ancient Egypt to the Present Day*, Hamlyn 1967
Cooke, P.C., *English Costume,* Gallery Press 1968
Courtais, G. de, *Women's Headdress and Hairstyles*, Batsford 1971
Cunningham, C.W., P.E., *Costume in Pictures,* Studio Vista 1964;
English Women's Clothing in the Present Century, Faber 1952
Cunnington, C.W., & Mansfield, *Handbook of English Costume in the 20th Century*, Faber 1970
Davenport, M., *The Book of Costume*, Bonanza 1968
DeAntfrasio, Charles & Roger, *History of Hair*, Bonanza 1970
Dorner, Jane, *Fashion*, Octopus 1974; *Fashion in the Twenties and Thirties*, Ian Allan 1973
Ewing, E., *History of Twentieth-Century Fashion*, Batsford 1974
Fairholt, F.W., *Costume in England*, G. Bell & Sons Ltd., 1885
Francoise, Lejeune, *Histoire du Costume*, Editions Delalain
Garland, M., *The Changing Face of Beauty*, Weidenfeld & Nicolson 1957;
History of Fashion, Orbis 1975
Gernsheim, Alison, *Fashion and Reality*, Faber 1963
Gorsline, D., *What People Wore*, Bonanza 1951
Gunn, Fenja, *The Artificial Face*, David and Charles 1973
Hansen, H., *Costume Cavalcade*, Methuen 1956
Harrison, Molly, *Hairstyles and Hairdressing*, Ward Lock 1968
Kelly, Mary, *On English Costume*, Deane 1934
Laver, James, *Concise History of Costume*, Thames & Hudson 1963;
Costume Through the Ages, Thames & Hudson 1964;
Dandies, Weidenfeld and Nicolson 1968; *Dress*, John Murray 1950;
Women's Dress in the Jazz Age, Hamish Hamilton 1964
Lister, Margot, *Costume*, Herbert Jenkins 1967
Moore, D., *Fashion Through Fashion Plates 1771-1970*, Ward Lock 1971
Norris, Herbert, *Costume and Fashion*, J.M. Dent 1924
Pistolese & Horstig, *History of Fashions*, Wiley 1970
Saint-Laurent, C., *History of Ladies Underwear*, Michael Joseph 1968
Schofield, Angela, *Clothes in History*, Wayland 1974
Streatfield, Noel, *Shoes*, Franklin Watts 1971
Truman, N., *Historic Costuming*, Pitman 1936
Waugh, N., *The Cut of Women's Clothes 1600-1930*, Faber 1968
Wilcox, R.T., *Dictionary of Costume*, Batsford 1970; *The Mode in Costume,*
Scribner's 1942; *The Mode in Hats and Headdress*, Scribner's 1948
Wilkerson, Marjorie, *Clothes*, Batsford 1970
Wilson, E., *History of Shoe Fashions*, Pitman 1969
Yarwood, D., *English Costume from the 2nd Century BC to the Present Day,*
Batsford 1975; *Outline of English Costume*, Batsford 1967
Pictorial Encyclopedia of Fashion, Hamlyn 1968

Index

Accessories 22, 48, 60
Afternoon dress 26, 27, 28, 31
Apron 27, 31
Armband 16, 42

Basque 32
Bathing costume 6, 18, 42
Bathing trunks 18
Beard 20
Beauty aid 21, 59
Belt 13, 14, 24, 26, 27, 31, 32, 33, 34, 36, 37, 40, 41, 42, 45, 46, 61
  half belt 14, 16, 32, 45
Beret 6, 37, 44, 51, 54, 55
Blazer 16, 17, 18, 42
Blouse 24, 27, 28, 32, 33, 34, 36, 37, 39, 41, 61
  jumper 33; tunic 34; shirt 33
Bodice 24, 26, 27, 28, 31, 39, 40, 41, 42, 43
Bolero 28, 32, 33, 37, 40
Boots 17, 18, 19, 42
  carriage 48; half 19; hooks 18; laces 18, 19; Russian 48; skating 45; top 17; Wellington 19
Bow tie 13, 15
Braces 9, 34
Brassière 42
Breeches 16, 17, 18, 42
Buckle 13, 26, 50, 61
Button 8, 9, 10, 12, 13, 14, 15, 16, 17, 18, 19, 22, 26, 28, 32, 37, 41, 43, 45, 46, 60, 62
  brace 9, 13; cuff 23; hole 8, 9, 10, 12, 13, 16; link 8, 9, 15; loop 46; stand 8

Camisole 45
Cane 22
Cap 17, 18, 20, 21, 43, 51, 54, 55
  bathing 43; Juliet 42, 55; skull 55
Cape 14, 28, 33, 40, 43, 60
Cardigan 17, 33, 36, 37, 43
Chignon 56
Cloak 40
Coat 6, 8, 9, 14, 19, 26, 27, 33, 34, 36, 37, 40, 41, 42, 43, 45, 46
  box 33, 46; Chesterfield 14, 46; covert 14; frock 41, 62; jigger 33; leather 18; motoring 4; Newbury 14; Raglan 14, 45, 46; swagger 6, 26, 33, 46; trench 4, 46; Ulster 14
Collar 8, 9, 12, 13, 14, 15, 16, 17, 26, 28, 31, 32, 33, 36, 37, 39, 40, 41, 43, 45, 46, 51, 61
  cape 31, 40, 46; double 13; high 16; Medici 28; Peter Pan 28; roll 15, 16, 17; sailor 26, 32; scarf 33, 34, 36, 46; separate 13; soft 13, stand 13, 34, 45; stand-fall 13; step 8, 9; stiff 22; stud 22; wing 13, 15
Costume 32, 41, 42
Cuff 8, 10, 11, 16, 28, 33, 39, 43, 45, 61
Cuff link 22
Cycle clips 17

Dirndl 31
Dress 24, 26, 28, 32, 33, 36, 37, 39, 40, 41, 42, 43, 45, 46, 60, 61, 62, 63, 64
Dress coat 14, 15, 16, 22
Dress suit 13, 16

Epaulette 40, 46
Eton crop 5, 24, 57
Evening dress 13, 26, 28, 39, 40, 41, 42
Evening wear 14, 21, 22, 23, 37, 39, 55, 57, 58, 60, 61
Eyebrow pencil 59
Facing 16
Fan 61
Fill-in 28, 31
Flannel trousers 16, 17
Flaps 10
Fly 9, 13, 14
Footwear 18, 19, 46, 48
Formal wear 5, 10, 14, 41
Frock coat 5, 8, 10, 12, 15, 16, 17
Frogging 16

Gaiters 17, 22
Galoshes 19
Garters 19, 45
Gloves 15, 16, 17, 18, 22, 42, 45, 48, 60
Gore 9, 24, 27

Hair 5, 19, 20, 43, 44, 52, 55, 56, 57, 58, 59, 63, 64
  ribbon 43, 64
Hairpiece 20, 56
Hairstyles 5, 19, 20, 24, 26, 56, 57, 58
  bob 5, 56, 58; shingle 5, 56, 57, 58
Handbag 37, 46, 48, 60
Handkerchief 9, 16, 22, 61
Hats 17, 18, 19, 20, 21, 26, 33, 51, 52, 53, 54, 55, 64
  boater 21; bowler 9, 21; Breton sailor 54, 55; cloche 24, 43, 45, 52, 53; Eden 21; felt 17, 21; hard 17; helmet 52, 53; Homburg 9, 21, 43; panama 21; picture 53; pillbox 6, 54; pork pie 21; silk 9; snap brim 5, 21; straw 18, 54; top 5, 9, 15, 17, 21; Trilby 5, 21; turban 54; Tyrolean 54
Headwear 6, 9, 20, 42, 51, 52, 55
Hood 14, 55

Hook and bar 9, 13, 60, 62
Housecoat 41
Housegown 41

Informal wear 10, 16, 42

Jabot 41, 61
Jacket 10, 11, 12, 15, 16, 17, 21, 24, 32, 33, 34, 40, 42, 43, 45
dinner 7, 13, 15; hacking 17; Norfolk 16, 17; pyjama 41; sports 16, 17; smoking 16; tailored 26; tweed 16, 17
Jersey 17, 33, 36, 43, 63
Jodhpurs 17, 42
Jumper 6, 24, 26, 27, 28, 32, 36, 37, 45, 64
dress 26, 32; suit 32; waistcoat 33

Knickerbockers 7, 17, 19
Knickers 42, 45
cami-knickers 45
Knitwear 36

Lapel 7, 8, 9, 10, 11, 12, 14, 15, 26, 32, 33
notched 9, 16; pointed 15; rolled 8, 10, 11, 12, 14, 15
Legwear 12
Link 32, 33
Lipstick 59
Lounge jacket 9, 10, 13, 15, 16, 17
Lounge suit 7, 9, 10, 21, 32

Mackintosh 14, 46
Marcel waves 20, 58
Mascara 59
Morning coat 5, 8, 9, 10, 12, 15, 16, 17, 21
Moustache 20
cup 21
Mudpack 21
Muff 60
foot 48

Neckerchief 28, 31
Neckwear 13

Oilskins 17
Outdoor wear 14, 45
Overcoat 32, 33, 45, 46
Overdress 26
Overskirt 18, 27, 39
Overtunic 26, 28, 39
Oxford bags 5, 7, 12

Panties 45
Parasol 61
Permanent wave 20, 58
Petticoat 41

Pinafore dress 28
Piping 10, 15
Playsuit 43
Pleat 9, 12, 16, 26, 27, 31, 32, 34, 39, 40, 41, 43, 45, 54
accordion 26, 27; box 34; inverted 14, 26, 34, 37; knife 34; side 34; sunray 43
Plimsolls 19
Plus fours 7, 17
Pocket 8, 9, 10, 14, 15, 16, 36, 43, 45, 46
breast 8, 10, 15, 16, 22, 61; flapped 10, 37; hip 10; patch 14, 16, 41, 42; slit 36; ticket 8, 10; trouser 14; vertical 14; waist 10
Powder 21, 59
Press stud 62
Pullover 16, 17, 45
Princess style 28, 41
Pyjamas 6
beach 43; suit 37, 40

Raincoat 6, 14, 46
Reefer
coat 10; jacket 10, 18, 33; suit 18
Rever 10, 26, 28, 33, 37, 39, 46

Sandals 19, 50, 63
Sash 24, 26, 31, 37, 39, 40, 41
Scarf 18, 22, 28, 34, 40, 46, 55, 57, 59, 61
Shawl 40, 60
Shift dress 31
Shirt 17, 18, 28, 32, 43
dress 28
Shoes 5, 6, 7, 18, 19, 22, 43, 46, 48, 49, 50, 51, 60
bows 19; brogues 18, 19; canvas 18; co-respondent 18; court 49, 50; monks 19; over- 19, 48; Oxford 19; pumps 19; sand 19; sports 19
Shorts 17, 18, 37, 42, 43
Side burns 20
Singeing 20
Skirt 5, 6, 8, 24, 26, 27, 28, 31, 32, 33, 34, 36, 37, 39, 40, 41, 42, 43, 45, 50, 63
divided 37, 43; harem 37; hobble 27; pencil 34; sheath 27
Slacks 43
Sleeves 8, 10, 11, 14, 26, 28, 31, 32, 33, 34, 37, 39, 40, 41, 42, 46
Bishop 31, 34, 46; cape 32, 40; Dolman 46; gigot 46; inset 26; kick-up 37; leg-o'-mutton 46; Magyar 27, 31, 36, 46; puffed 26, 28, 32, 37; Raglan 14, 26, 31, 36, 46; shirt 11

Slipper 50
Slits 14, 16, 17
Smock 31
Snood 6, 55, 59
Socks 19, 43, 45, 63
Sou'wester 53
Spats 15, 16, 18, 22
Sports wear 16, 37, 42, 46
Stiffener 13
Stockings 17, 18, 43, 45, 49, 60
Stole 60
Strap and buckle 9, 12, 15, 19, 22
Strap and loop 13
Suit 10, 12, 16, 18, 21, 32, 33, 34, 36, 37, 45, 63
cocktail 41; jacket 36, 61; tailored 24, 32, 36
Suspender belt 45
Suspenders 19
Sweater 5, 7, 16, 17, 18

Tail coat 14, 15, 17
Tailor-made 6, 26, 32, 61
Tails 8, 9, 14
Tie 7, 13, 15, 16, 17, 18, 22, 34
four-in-hand 13
Tie pin 22
Toupée 20
Trousers 5, 7, 9, 10, 12, 13, 15, 16, 17, 18, 19, 21, 37, 43, 45, 63
suit 37, 40; Turkish 37
Tunic 27, 42
Turban 6, 55, 56
Turn-ups 19, 37, 43
Turtle neck 16
Twin set 6, 36

Umbrella 22, 61
Under garment 45
Under skirt 26
Under tunic 45
Underwear 45

Veil 42, 54, 55
Vent
back 8, 9, 10, 16; centre 8, 10, 17

Waistcoat 5, 7, 8, 9, 10, 12, 13, 14, 15, 16, 26, 33, 36, 37
knitted 17
Walking stick 15, 16, 22
Watch
pocket 22; wrist 22
Whiskers 20

Yoke 16, 27, 28, 31, 34, 37, 39

Zip 13, 17, 37, 41, 60, 62